D1145967

I've Said It Before...

I've Said It Before...

UNPUBLISHED LETTERS TO THE
Daily Mail

Compiled and edited by
ANDY SIMPSON

Constable • London

Constable & Robinson Ltd
55–56 Russell Square
London WC1B 4HP
www.constablerobinson.com

First published in the UK by Constable,
an imprint of Constable & Robinson Ltd, 2011

A copy of the British Library Cataloguing in
Publication Data is available from the British Library

ISBN: 978-1-78033-112-6

Typeset by TW Typesetting, Plymouth, Devon

Printed and bound in the UK

1 3 5 7 9 10 8 6 4 2

PEFC
PEFC/16-33-111
CATG-PEFC-052
www.pefc.org

Contents

Contents

Introduction

To those who aren't in the know, writing a letter to the *Daily Mail* may seem like turning into 'Disgusted of Tunbridge Wells', but the breadth of this collection shows just how eclectic and varied the *Daily Mail* readership is.

From politics and culture, to sport, media and history, our readers have an opinion on everything; and by letter, fax or email they endeavour to be heard. Deep philosophical musings, barbed critiques and humorous asides, which all make up the fabric of the *Daily Mail*'s Readers' Letters page, come from all ends of the country – even Tunbridge Wells, Llandrindod Wells, Pannanich Wells and Struell Wells.

Although the *Daily Mail* does dedicate more space to Readers' Letters than any other national newspaper, we can't publish all the marvellous letters we receive and there are many would-be contributors who don't quite make it into the paper. We have produced here, for your education and entertainment, a dedicated selection of their intelligence, feeling, experience, insight and wit, as a token of our appreciation for the many letters received each week.

Andy Simpson, Readers' Letters editor

All at sea

The navy lark

What sort of navy have we got these days? I had a good laugh at HMS *Manchester*, in the Caribbean, failing to sink what appeared to be an unmanned, motionless, fibreglass motor boat at reasonably short range, on a calm sea, using a four-and-a-half-inch gun and heavy machine gun, etc.

Next, they put a matelot armed with an axe and handsaw on board, who attacked the bottom of the boat – but still it wouldn't sink. So they tried pouring petrol and igniting it. And all this was on 21 October – enough to make Lord Nelson (God rest him) turn in his tomb.

How will they manage when a suicide boat, laden with explosives, approaches at full speed?

Mr N. S. Nevard, Orpington, Kent

To the enormous relief of the Admiralty, my mates and I have saved the Royal Navy from the embarrassment of having two shiny new multibillion pound aircraft carriers but no aircraft. In true Dunkirk spirit, every member of our local microlight aircraft club has volunteered to fly his 'trike' off the navy's mighty 60,000 ton carriers – and it's more than likely that the guys from Little Snodingham's club will join us, making nine planes in all.

What a stirring sight and sound that will be – our little two-stroke engines buzzing like a swarm of angry lawnmowers as the colourful wire and fabric contraptions leap from the heaving deck of the *Queen Elizabeth* and soar skywards to strike fear into the hearts of Britain's enemies. If the sheer spectacle of these avenging butterflies does not terrify any pestilential terrorists, we might paint threatening slogans under our wings or tow banners saying, 'Go Away!' or 'Stop that immediately!'

If we meet an especially recalcitrant enemy, our brave pilots will buzz them (at their maximum speed of forty-five miles per hour), shake their fists and glare fiercely. Naturally, the lethal weaponry carried by these 'trikes' is a state secret but if I mention the code words 'custard pies' and 'rotten eggs' you'll get some idea of the immense embarrassment these little planes can cause.

So, just as the 'little ships' rescued the British army at Dunkirk, these 'little planes' will save the Royal Navy from becoming an international laughing stock.

David H. Lewis, Caerphilly, South Wales

If I were the President of Argentina, I'd make an offer our cash-strapped government couldn't refuse for the aircraft carrier *Ark Royal* and its Harriers, along with a few low-mileage frigates and destroyers, and park them off the Falklands Islands.

John Wright, Duston, Northamptonshire

Having lived through the whole Cold War, I never thought that I would raise three cheers for the Russians – for the robust way in which they tackled the Somali pirates. Lessons to be relearned?

John Dixon, Tewkesbury, Gloucestershire

Admiral Horatio Nelson was dead before the Battle of Trafalgar was won. It was his second in command, Vice Admiral Lord Cuthbert Collingwood who was the master of naval gunnery – with three broadsides every three and a half minutes, which was never equalled.

Collingwood took command and successfully annihilated the Spanish and beat the part of the French fleet that was at Trafalgar. Between 1805 and 1810, Collingwood defeated the remainder of the French navy before he died on his way home.

England desperately needed a hero in 1805 and Nelson-mania took hold after the pamphleteers – the spin-doctors of their day – took control.

The long chase across the Atlantic that preceded Trafalgar was a ruse by Napoleon. He ordered the French admiral Villeneuve to take the French fleet to the West Indies knowing that a large part of the blockade would follow. The weather, however, prevented Villeneuve from returning in time for the planned invasion of England and Napoleon went for Austria instead. Villeneuve knew he was to be replaced and decided to set out from Cadiz before it happened. France and Spain were now fighting the Royal Navy at Trafalgar and the rest is history, as they say.

As far as Nelson was concerned, he wasn't very good at taking orders (as the battles of Calvi, Santa Cruz and

Copenhagen bear witness). Was he a hero? We all know how heroes are better reported on once they're dead.

Edmund Futers, Chipping Campden, Gloucestershire

HMS *Victory* in Portsmouth Dockyard is still a commissioned warship. If the Royal Navy has to share ships with the French, will the French sailors occupy the fore or aft of this vessel?

E. Barker, Southampton, Hampshire

It's comforting to learn that, should I ever be lost at sea, I might be rescued by none other than Prince William in his See King helicopter.

Frank Skorrow, Barnsley, South Yorkshire

Prince William is on record as saying that he would fight for his country – but would he fight for the Americans?

Gareth Boote, Leigh, Lancashire

Life on the ocean wave

After making a few calculations, we've decided never to go into a care home – we're going on a cruise instead.

The average cost of a care home is about £69 a day. A cruise-liner berth, over a long period, with senior citizens' reductions, works out at about £47 a day, leaving us with roughly £22 a day, which can be spent on drinks and tips.

Drinks are only about £8 a day. You can have up to ten free

lunches a day if you want to stay and gorge in the restaurant or you can use room service and have lunch in bed every day. Cruise ships have swimming pools, a gymnasium, a laundry service and there's entertainment every evening.

The cabin bathroom is provided with free dentifrice, razors, soap and shampoo, and clean sheets and towels appear daily without you having to ask. The crew will treat you as a client, not a number. If you tip them about £5 a day, they will look after you very well.

Your phone breaks down? A lamp blows? Your mattress needs changing? No problem: there will always be someone to put it right and to apologise for the inconvenience.

If you fall and hurt yourself, instead of having to rely on the NHS, you'll be treated on board and probably get a better cabin for the rest of your life. And if you die on board, you can be buried at sea at no additional cost.

You'll meet new people about every seven or ten days. Meanwhile, you get to visit South America, Panama, Tahiti, Australia, New Zealand, Asia, etc.

So when I've got my pension, don't go looking for me in a care home.

T. H. Southgate, Cheadle Hulme, Cheshire

It's a mistake to think that there are no recorded incidents of pirates attempting to board a cruise ship. On Saturday, 25 April 2010 at 23.30, MSC *Melody* came under attack from Somali pirates about 150 miles north of the Seychelles.

The pirates made a strong, prolonged attempt to board the vessel from the starboard aft side, using lightweight ladders from a small boat. The next morning, our captain claimed that the crew had repulsed the pirates but in fact they were driven off by passengers who, disturbed during a balmy Indian Ocean evening on the aft deck, threw tables and sun loungers at them.

The pirates weren't impressed and steered away at high speed, firing AK-47s at the ship. The pirate vessel rounded the ship's stern and raked it from stern to stem on the port side, firing numerous rounds that smashed windows and punched holes through the ship's steel-plated side.

My wife and I were sitting in the piano bar after ordering fresh drinks when the bullets started to whizz through the bar. We were ordered back to our cabin before we could finish our drinks, which we'd already signed for. I'm still annoyed that the Captain didn't replace my malt whisky the next day.

Anthony Coleman, Canvey Island, Essex

Rail and road

On the right track?

The professor who was fined £155 for leaving a train early had no excuse and I propose that similar punitive fines should be made mandatory in all circumstances, including: leaving a theatre or cinema before the end of the performance; leaving a sports ground before the end of the match; removing a vehicle from a car park before the ticket has expired; vacating a hotel room before check-out time; leaving a stately home before viewing all of the rooms; leaving a theme park before completing all of the rides; leaving a zoo before seeing all of the animals; returning a rowing boat within the hour; and vacating a deckchair prematurely.

The professor is fortunate in having made at least part of his journey. He would presumably have received a considerably higher fine had he failed to use his ticket at all.

David Birnie, St Ives, Cambridgeshire

I sympathise with the disabled lady who has to travel twenty extra miles by train just to be able to cross the twenty yards to the opposite platform. Some years ago, I was travelling from London to Staplehurst, Kent, by train and knew I would have to travel on to Ashford to cross the line by lift and then back to Staplehurst as my daughter was in a disabled travelling buggy.

After a long day at a London hospital, however, I couldn't face the thought of an extra hour's travel and decided to attempt to drag the buggy up the stairs myself.

On reaching the stairs, I realised my mistake: I wasn't physically strong enough to do it. As I stood and thought about my dilemma, the train driver left his cab, picked up both buggy and child and climbed the stairs and crossed the bridge. I never wrote a letter of thanks to the train company as the driver might have been in serious trouble but I remain very grateful.

Mrs Margaret Boutell, Northiam, East Sussex

I watched Jeremy Clarkson take his ride on the steam engine *Tornado* from London to Edinburgh. I imagine it must have been a very unusual trip for him and very dirty compared with the cars he's used to. There were five men on the footplate, including three firemen, so Jeremy had a few rests.

There's nothing to compare with those big steam engines and no comparison anywhere else to the smell of steam and oil. I lived in Crewe, Cheshire, where engines were designed and built, and worked from 1947, firing all types of steam engines. I fired them from Crewe to London, Glasgow and many other places. In those days, there were just two of us on the footplate – the driver and the fireman – and on those trips to Glasgow and on to Perth, I shovelled ten tons of coal.

Nobody these days knows what ten tons means – only a fireman knows, and he alone notices if it's good coal or not, the difference making a journey easier, or terrible.

The only food we had on those trips was sandwiches, covered

from the coal dust flying around in the cab. And when it was time to eat, there was nowhere to wash our hands. There were no toilets either – don't ask.

The *Tornado* is new and was very clean compared with the filthy engines I knew, but I was used to it and loved it all. My father worked there for forty-nine years. In 1936 he fired the Royal Train from Crewe to Carlisle and was given ten shillings (fifty pence) for shovelling all the way.

Geoff Hillyard, Sandbach, Cheshire

The ninth 'most charismatic' railway line in the country was listed as the Blackpool to Preston and Colne line. This should read Blackpool to Preston and Leeds (or more accurately between Burnley and Halifax), taking in the Copy Pit line through the South Pennines and running from Burnley through to Hebden Bridge, with its original station signs and flower decorations.

Burnley has enough bad press. This section of the line runs through the Calder Valley, once home to a rich industrial heritage, nestled deep within the South Pennines. This is still evident, with former quaint textile communities juxtaposed against the backdrop of the famous and spectacular Cliviger Gorge. I live in Burnley, just a few metres from the line and regularly use it to commute to work in West Yorkshire. The wonderful South Pennines is rich in wildlife and industrial heritage.

Dr Martyn Walker, Burnley, Lancashire

A couple of years ago, I took my long-suffering wife on a railway tour of Scotland, the itinerary of which was as follows:

Glasgow to Fort William, passing alongside the Clyde, turning north via Gairloch and then overlooking Loch Lomond;

Fort William to Mallaig and over the Glenfinnan Viaduct now made famous by the Harry Potter film;

A short ferry journey to Skye and a bus ride to Kyle of Lochalsh, and then back on the train to Inverness – surely the most picturesque railway journey in the country;

Inverness to Edinburgh, through Blair Atholl, Kingussie, Aviemore, and eventually over the magnificent Forth Bridge – in close second place for the picturesque railway journey.

We had probably travelled along four of the top half-dozen best routes in the country.

Chris Pate, Worcester

The other day my seventeen-year-old son booked and under-took a 170-mile train journey through France. Unfortunately, due to a train breakdown, a connection was missed, which meant he had a two-hour wait at the station. Nothing unusual in this, except while the ticket cost only €24, because the connection was missed a three-course restaurant meal was provided by the French rail authorities to all affected passengers.

Do British railway operators have similar contingency plans?

Mike Sinstadt, France

Risking the road

Tony Blair used to like to appoint a 'tsar' to overcome any problem. To tackle road congestion, should we have a 'Tsar of all the Rush Hours'?

Eveleigh Moore Dutton, Malpas, Cheshire

I travel from Brentwood to Hemel Hempstead each day on the M25 and M1 and am amazed by the things I see. I believe I can disprove the theory that drivers exhibit a specific kind of behaviour if they drive a certain type of car.

In one week, I've seen too many lorry and car drivers texting to count, a woman in a sports car, with her baby next to her, reading a document balanced on the steering wheel, many motorists drinking coffee or on the phone, one dozing off, drivers pulling in front of me to gain just one space when I've been trying to leave a safe distance, many people lane-dodging without indicating – and most of this happening at more than sixty miles per hour.

In that week, I've seen too many accidents to count, one happening right in front of me, and the motorway has been closed at least twice.

My office is now relocating to Ipswich so it's the A12 for me, where the lanes are narrow but drivers happily do ninety miles per hour. I only hope I won't end up in a body bag through somebody else's selfishness.

Sherri Fraser, Brentwood, Essex

Surely, like me, the thousands of people who had to queue for upwards of three hours, just to pay the toll on the QE-II Bridge, think toll roads do not work in the UK. Goodness knows how much fuel was wasted in each of the thousands of cars, vans and trucks, just to pay a silly tax.

What, I wonder, would be the impact if those thousands of people sued the government for the costs of these wanton delays to their journeys.

Gordon Scott, Kempshott, Hampshire

Right royal trad

Doing a good job

It has been suggested that the Queen could save money by shopping at Tesco. About twenty years ago, while I was buying petrol, a very distinctive limousine pulled in behind me and I noticed police motorcyclists preventing other vehicles from entering or leaving the forecourt. The absence of number plates on the car confirmed almost immediately that this was the Queen's Rolls-Royce.

Sadly, the Queen wasn't on board, but I learnt later that the car was being fuelled in preparation for a royal visit the following day. This happened at Tesco at Five Ways, Edgbaston, where the petrol was the cheapest in the area by some margin. This episode always comes to mind when Her Majesty's apparent frugality is mentioned.

Mark Barrett, West Bromwich, West Midlands

Anyone confused about which £20 note is legal tender should wait for the next new one. On the back is a smiling Lord Prescott wearing a crown with matching robes and a mace. There are two Jaguars parked on a croquet lawn in the background.

On the front, replacing the Queen, is Lady Prescott under a hair dryer, reading *Hello!* magazine.

Dave Warner, Market Harborough, Leicestershire

Who's next?

The Queen has done a magnificent job since taking the throne fifty-nine years ago but is it not time for her to retire and let Charles, her eldest son and heir, take the reins, so to speak, and do the job that he has been trained to do for the best part of his life?

There are lots of people in this country who think he's not right for the job but personally I think he should be given the chance, which might well be his last one.

The Queen is eighty-four and starting to show signs of wear and tear – wouldn't it be a good time for her to stand down in favour of her son now?

Yvonne Embery, Bristol

Those who advocate that Prince Charles does his duty and stands down as our next king in favour of his son, Prince William, may be in the majority but, alas, it will never happen.

If nothing else, our constitutional monarchy is steeped in tradition. Our present queen is never likely to stand down, nor should she, so hopefully she'll be with us, for many years to come. It's highly unlikely that the idea of standing aside from accepting the crown, after waiting for it all his life, has ever occurred to Charles, or been discussed in court circles.

The most those of us who remember the appalling treatment Princess Diana received at the hands of this couple can hope for is that the reign of Charles III and 'Queen' Camilla will be reduced to a minimum by old age.

Alan Berry, Camberley, Surrey

Why exactly should William be the next king? Prince Charles is next in line and should be king in due course. Why ever not? He's happily married, intelligent, has a lively mind and will make an excellent king.

William is still an unknown quantity. Charles at the same age was just as popular. When Charles and Diana married the press was just as ecstatic as at the present royal marriage. There are no guarantees as to how the Will and Kate marriage will work out. To sideline Charles is terribly unfair. Leave the man alone.

So Prince Charles hasn't always been a saint? Which Prince of Wales ever has? The succession is not a popularity contest; while Charles may have some unpopular opinions, at least he does have opinions and an active brain. I wish him well and feel it would be a great loss to the nation if he were excluded from the succession. Please, God, may it never happen.

Rochelle C. Jones, Camborne, Cornwall

As I understand the hereditary principle, if Prince Charles never becomes king of England, his elder son, Prince William, will never be the rightful heir to the throne. So if for some reason Charles fails to succeed his mother (the reigning monarch), the next in line would be the older of his two brothers, Prince Andrew.

However, should a majority of the UK electorate decide that they want to choose their titular head of state by bovine popular demand, we might as well go the whole hog and let Simon Cowell and Piers Morgan turn the whole shooting match into an all-singing, all-dancing game show.

'Ladies and gentlemen, coming to a TV screen somewhere near you, some time soon, the Banal British Crass Media unashamedly presents: *The Rex Factor!*'

Jim Price, Luton, Bedfordshire

Charlie boy

If Prince Charles, his brothers, sister or any of his family attended our local primary and comprehensive schools, they would probably be in the below-average set. Their grades would be so low that they would probably not make it to university or, if they did, it would be an inferior university.

I suspect that, had they not been born into royalty, they wouldn't even aspire to the position of their own staff.

My children and most of the village children who attended these schools – with none of the advantages of private education, best tutors and fiddled exam results – gained high GCSE and A-level passes and went on to good universities to do BAs, MAs and PhDs.

Sandra Johnson, Mouldsworth, Cheshire

What would have become of Prince Charles if he didn't have royal status? My contacts with him have left me of the opinion that on his own he would probably have succeeded in becoming at least a billionaire.

Having had personal experience of his kindness and courtesy

in connection with charities and seeing him play polo with hair-raising courage, I have the highest possible opinion of his capacity for hard work and attention to detail. In addition, he seems to have a mind-set comparable to the great philanthropists in England and America who used their millions to set up structures that benefited whole sections of the population, many of which still exist as world-famous museums, public works, etc.

Dr Margery Williams, Holworth, Dorset

Duchess or Queen?

A queen by any other name . . . it doesn't really matter what we want to call Camilla, when Prince Charles becomes king she will be his queen.

At the moment he is the Prince of Wales, so technically she is the Princess of Wales. He cares about so many issues and now he has the right lady by his side. So let's leave them in peace.

Jo Coley, Minster on Sea, Kent

I noted that the Duchess of Cornwall had a stopover in Bangalore before attending the opening of the Commonwealth Games. I wish I'd known she was visiting Bangalore as she could have done me the favour of visiting the many call centres there and, on my behalf, given them a bit of a rollicking. That's if they could understand her as most of them fail to comprehend any point I'm making, sidetrack anything I ask and usually provide incorrect information.

Alan Cairns, Tadley, Hampshire

his 'job' as a trade representative was about anything other than lining his own pocket and behaving badly? What a despicable bunch they all are – yet we put up with it. Disgraceful!

Carole Sampson, Chelmsford, Essex

The case of the eleven-year-old who travelled 150 miles to see the Queen at Buckingham Palace regarding his bullying misery, could have been better handled. What a golden opportunity to show the caring side of the monarchy.

For a child, bullying is often a personal nightmare, leading to absenteeism, leaving home, even suicide. The palace lackey who simply said, 'Her Majesty has not been made aware of this case but I am sure she would be very concerned', exhibited breathtaking intransigence. If he was so sure, why didn't he tell the Queen and let the her make up her own mind?

Palace officials should stop shielding the Queen from the basic, colder aspects of street-life. Given just a few minutes of Her Majesty's time, this brave boy could have gained a memory not of a remote figure, clueless about her subjects' daily trials and tribulations, but of someone who really cared.

Mr J. Cole, Southsea, Hampshire

There are increasing calls for higher minimum alcohol prices in the hope of curbing binge drinking – but we all know this will have little effect.

What might really help would be for young members of the royal family to set a better example to the young and perhaps even head an advertising campaign for moderation.

Barney Russell, Colchester, Essex

Royalty has a long tradition of playboys and womanisers, including Charles II, George IV and his brothers, Edward VII and Edward VIII. Prince Harry is a young man who fights for his country, cares about the less fortunate and enjoys clubbing and beautiful girlfriends. What's wrong with that?

Mark Taha, London SE26

Well done, Your Majesty! Someone had to stop the liberal rot in this country and there's no one better than you. You had the guts to stand up and be counted, to express your personal Christian beliefs in your Christmas message and how much they mean to your life.

Take note, you wishy-washy churchmen and women, liberal politicians, teachers and social workers who believe in everything but have convictions about nothing.

Her Majesty's attitude will do more to arrest the moral and spiritual decline in this country than any churchman or politician has done in the last twenty years or more.

Simon Icke, Aston Clinton, Buckinghamshire

The Queen does not command universal respect. She must be the most materialistic woman in Britain. She stood with her daughter and actually wept when her precious yacht was taken away, notwithstanding her umpteen sumptuous palaces and castles – and she still doesn't even pay her full amount of tax.

She has no sense of morality, having encouraged her son Charles's infidelity from the time of his honeymoon. She could have stopped it if it wasn't for the good old Duke.

Whilst her daughter was still married, she encouraged her

infidelity with another, inviting him to picnics at Balmoral. And she allowed her younger son to live under her roof with his girlfriend.

She has the effrontery to stand in front of us and talk of her faith and Christian values. Talk is all it is: I doubt if she has ever done a good or generous deed for anyone.

J. Wakeham, Norwich, Norfolk

I can't understand the 'concern' over the royal family, in particular Prince Andrew. I appreciate he has to use good judgement in his public life but he's a middle-aged, divorced man. He's not going to be king and he's no longer restricted by life in the Royal Navy. He's fully entitled to enjoy himself now, including exotic holidays and attractive female company.

The nation can't ask the Royal Family to 'lighten up' and then criticise them when they do.

Mel Patten, Crewkerne, Somerset

I sympathise with the woman who was on the receiving end of the Princess Royal's bad temper. But, believe me, it was nothing compared with what her father, Prince Philip, said to me when he and the Queen visited Birmingham in the 1960s.

Unfortunately, as the royal car slowed down to take a corner someone pushed me and my little girl from behind straight into its path. Both the Queen and Prince were standing up but if anyone was in danger it was my little girl and me. The profanity uttered by the Prince was heard all around.

The incident was not reported in the newspapers but since

then I have never bothered with any royal visit. Princess Diana's good grace and courtesy would have shamed the lot of them.

Mrs Monica Reynolds, Bournemouth, Dorset

I once came unexpectedly face to face with Princess Anne and I'm sorry to say she was horrid. I was staying with an old school chum at her cottage in a Cotswold village.

Despite severe arthritis she had gone to a lot of trouble to make a custard tart and had put it on the open window ledge to cool.

We heard the clatter of hooves in the road outside, followed by a loud crash and a howl of rage. One of her dogs had jumped up and was gobbling the pie. 'Bloody stupid place to put that,' said a furious Anne who glared back at me as I stared outside, open-mouthed.

Then she gave her horse a whack and rode off without even a muttered 'Sorry'.

Phillipa Kelsall, Leek, Staffordshire

A class of loving, caring, country children was invited to share in the visit of Princess Anne to the local US Air Force base at Lakenheath. Edward, aged eight, brought for the Princess a dewy bunch of small lavender irises, which he called 'lilacs'. We all know the look in a trusting child's eyes.

In the event, the car windows stayed closed for safety reasons and Edward came back with his flowers, his face a picture of woe. I promised him that she would get them.

I wrote a letter on a piece of paper, with a crossed nib, telling her about this, and pointed out that the flowers were 'lilacs'.

Almost too late, the whole village became involved. One of the mothers wrapped up the wet parcel. The post office stayed open for it and the postmaster took it to Shetford to catch the London train.

Princess Anne wrote a beautiful letter back, which Edward always cherished. It was a personal letter, in which the irises were lilacs.

To me, then and forever, I know of her heart.

Celia Burgan, Sheffield

When my mother was recovering from a fall in Middlesex Hospital, Princess Anne was due to open a ward there. Huge bouquets of flowers suddenly appeared on every ward and the red carpet was duly unrolled.

When asked if any of the patients would like to be taken along to see the Princess, everyone (my mother included) refused. Had it been Princess Diana their beds would have been vacated like a shot in the rush to see her. Anne should lighten up or get a proper job.

L. Smith, Hove, East Sussex

Too many people don't understand how 'Auld Lang Syne' should be performed. The royal family, with their deep Scottish connections, know full well that hands should not be crossed at the start of the song.

The Queen is perfectly conversant with 'Auld Lang Syne' but was surprised that her prime minister, Tony Blair, obviously didn't know what was correct. Arms are crossed only with the words 'And here's a hand my trusty friend'.

Margaret Johnson, Tadworth, Surrey

Through the airwaves

What ho, the Home Service?

Now that Caroline Spelman is no longer selling off our forests, perhaps David Cameron could appoint her to thin out the dead wood at the BBC, especially as an awful lot of it is leaning dangerously to the left.

Brenda Michael, Crawley, West Sussex

I didn't expect to be jealous of those trapped Chilean miners but at least they got to see their national football team. We Freeview customers didn't even get extended highlights of England's match.

The BBC, uniquely funded by me (which is why I can't afford any other deals) didn't put it on.

Dave Blackman, Sidcup

The BBC dumbing down Radio 4? Never! Didn't I hear the Corporation is after Posh 'n' Becks to present *The Today Programme*, Coleen for *Woman's Hour* and Wayne for *In Our Time*? And how about Cheryl for *Thinking Aloud*?

Bryan Greene, Hedge End, Southampton

I hear that old episodes of the BBC radio series *Dick Barton, Special Agent* have been found in Australia. I hope they haven't found *Mrs Dale's Diary* as well.

Philip Brannon, London SE25

Why does the BBC insist on using the metric system, even when it's totally inappropriate? In a disappointing programme about Robert Stephenson, the building of a railway line in about 1840 was described using metres and kilometres, etc. This was completely out of line and spoiled the atmosphere. As with an earlier programme about the Spitfire, at the time of this aircraft such measurements simply were not used – the imperial system of feet, inches and miles was correct.

For several years it has been obvious that the BBC has sent out an edict: every programme, without question, must have metric measurements, including those produced by outside bodies. The BBC seems to have decided that all measurements should be metric, without any concern for the nature of the programme or the audience.

As an older person it's frustrating and I have to translate the measurements from metric back to imperial (how many acres in a hectare?) to make any sense. Come on BBC, let's have some flexibility in how you measure things.

A. J. Davis, Cambridge

Shopkeepers were being taken to court by the Trading Standards authorities for selling food in pounds and ounces while BBC news presenters were explaining that a regular colleague was missing because he had just become the father of a new baby – which weighed in at 'seven pounds eight ounces'. Nice one, Auntie Beeb!

Ian Bevan, Somerset

I pay £145.50 for a TV licence and the BBC airs a repeat showing of *Rip Off Britain* during peak viewing times (7.30 p.m. on a Thursday). Is this what's meant by irony?

Arthur Stradling, Conwy

I heard two presenters on local radio the other morning discussing a newspaper article that said the worst part of the week was Tuesday at 10 a.m. as this was when people actually start work.

One presenter said that she agreed because Monday is spent catching up with colleagues about the weekend and it isn't until Tuesday morning that she actually gets round to doing anything.

The second presenter said that Friday was also a good day because everybody is winding down for the weekend, to which the first presenter replied that she always does the winding down on Thursday as well – leaving just two days for any work to be done.

Could this be why the BBC costs so much to run?

Ruby Dowling, Bristol

It was good to see Max Clifford on the BBC news attacking alleged phone hacking. The last thing we need is people's dirty washing being hung out in public.

Bob Woodland, Poole, Dorset

What's on the box?

It's suggested that *The X Factor* contestants have no talent because they don't write their own songs. Does this mean Frank Sinatra had no talent? Or Dusty Springfield? Elvis Presley? Or, more recently, Susan Boyle?

They can't have, because they never wrote their songs. Nonsense. Their view was: 'You write a good song, which *you're* good at, and I'll sing it well, which *I'm* good at'. Better to be very good at one thing rather than quite good at a few.

David Haig, Poynton, Cheshire

I wonder what might have happened if the young John, George, Paul and Ringo had attended auditions for *The X Factor*. Would we have been deprived of one of the best groups ever?

M. Richards, Chatham, Kent

I was amused to see Carroll Levis referred to as the greatest talent-spotter of them all. After all, did he not reject the greatest band in history . . .The Beatles?

Robert Evans, Upton, Wirral

Why should James Shields playing the clarinet on *Britain's Got Talent* have been regarded as performing with an 'unfashionable' instrument? What makes such an instrument unfashionable? It's only because programmes such as this never include a clarinet, a trumpet, a trombone or even a piano. There are plenty of highly talented players of these instruments in Britain but the average television viewer never gets to see the likes of Alan Barnes or Julian Marc Stringle, for instance.

Why, for that matter, shouldn't jazz become popular again? Nobody puts players like this in a mainstream TV show, that's why.

Pete Godfrey, jazz piano player, Sompting, Sussex

The Brit Awards – the sparsely talented, accompanied by the scarcely intelligible.

R. Richardson, St Bees, Cumbria

We're asked to believe that *Britain's Got Talent* holds the same sort of attraction for twenty-first century viewers as that which lured the ancient Romans to the Colosseum to watch Christians being torn apart by lions.

The essential difference here is that the Christians were not volunteers which, one assumes, participants on *BGT* are.

Richard Okill, Lee-on-the-Solent, Hampshire

I was unfortunate to see a glimpse of Sam Fox being forced to eat something that looked inedible on *I'm A Celebrity* ... before flipping channels. It occurred to me in the light of the problem of bullying in schools, this was surely a clear case of bullying in the name of entertainment.

It could be argued that Ms Fox is a willing participant in the action and it was her attempt to resurrect her career and gain some kind of notoriety/popularity. If a child at school was doing what his/her 'friends' asked in order to gain popularity, it could be seen as the beginning of a slow slide into bullying.

The Sam Fox episode is tantamount to condoning bullying, and leaves one wondering how far we can push this kind of practice purely for the gratification of the viewing public.

Ronald Josland, Strood, Kent

I congratulate the production team and cast on an excellent episode of *Doctor Who* but am disappointed that a kissogram has been introduced as the Doctor's new companion.

While it can be argued that for the younger children watching Amy Pond was 'just dressing up', it still causes awkward questions for parents of older children and need not have been in the show.

The Doctor's previous companions have been scientists, journalists and an air stewardess. What happened to giving little girls positive role models to look up to, rather than glamorizing something that cheapens femininity?

Anthony Andrews, Fareham, Hampshire

Michael Winner tells us that he dines in the best restaurants and is a critic of most of them, but judging by his performance on *Dining Stars*, I suggest he asks Sir Roger Moore to instruct him in the correct handling of a soup spoon.

Mrs Mary Gunn, Shrewsbury, Shropshire

There's a lot to be said for the servant's life at *Downton Abbey*. In November 1945, I was in the RAF square-bashing at nearby Greenham Common.

Once a week, parading early on the cold windswept runway, we were assigned to fatigues. 'Any volunteers?' called Sergeant Palmer and – despite the 'don't volunteer for anything' received wisdom – I stepped forward to at least get warm by working. With two others, we were assigned to the officers' mess and were driven several miles to the tradesmen's entrance of the vast mansion.

We had to wash a few dishes and peel spuds but below stairs was wonderfully warm and at lunchtime the food was magnificent, compared with the austerity everyone else experienced.

The following week, when fatigues came up again, we were quick to volunteer but the sergeant had something new in mind. Soon, we were shovelling tons of coke. *Per ardua ad astra.*

John Nye, Tunbridge Wells, Kent

Why do nature programmes on television always have to feature a 'celebrity' presenter? An anonymous voice-over is adequate. In a programme such as *Islands of Britain*, the islands are so beautiful they almost speak for themselves (if they could they would say, 'Clear off, Martin Clunes.').

The ubiquity of celebrities is an annoyance to many people and an irrelevance to these programmes.

Antony Dean, Pudsey, Leeds

Regrettably, my children have been kidnapped and I've been told that unless I pay £1 million they'll be killed within twenty-four hours. I don't have that sort of money.

Luckily, I've found a man who knows where they're being held. However, even when I say 'pretty please' he won't disclose the details, so I wished him a very good afternoon and sent him on his way.

Now . . . what's on television tonight?

Peter Cohen, Eastbourne

Up on the soap box

I have neither the time nor the inclination to watch soaps on television but I chanced to stay with friends and out of courtesy sat down with them one evening when they wanted to watch *EastEnders*.

Being out of context for me, the story meant nothing so I was able to watch the actors objectively – more importantly, the characters. Though appalled, out of politeness to my hosts I made no comment. If folks want to watch garbage such as this then each to his own but if this is typical of programmes being beamed into the nation's homes every night then small wonder the boorishness and lack of manners in British people today.

The BBC should be ashamed to produce tripe such as this. From when my mother used to watch *Coronation Street* forty-odd years ago, I seem to recall at least some grace, humour, politeness and respect. This ghastly show lacked all of these. 'Coarseness' is the best word to describe the whole tone of the relationships between virtually all of the characters portrayed. Perhaps I was unfortunate and caught a bad script but when Barbara Windsor showed up, I lost all interest in living. This one-time gangster's moll, who I had assumed had been relegated to the dustbin of history, now appears to be regarded as a national treasure . . . which says all we need to know about our dumbed-down society in Britain today.

W. N. Robbins, Oswestry, Shropshire

The TV soaps are becoming a complete bore and are in need of a major change. *EastEnders* is a very morbid programme that certainly doesn't cheer anyone up. Over Christmas it made you cry when you would like to have a happy Christmas.

Coronation Street is running out of ideas – it's becoming a constant family crisis, with everyone having an affair. *Emmerdale*, too, is running out of material, causing complete boredom.

The worst aspect is that the storyline in each of these programmes revolves around public houses – there's hardly a single night's viewing when someone isn't in the pub. Our real lives don't revolve around the pub all the time. How much longer have we got to put up with these programmes?

Mr R. R. Hutchins, Totton, Southampton

Fifty years ago, on 9 December 1960, I made myself comfortable ready to watch a new programme called *Coronation Street*. I had not long been married and had read a lot about this new programme. Little did I know that I would still be watching fifty years later, still married to the same person I hasten to add. I have lapsed sometimes, but have always gone back to it.

I would like to congratulate the cast, writers and crew for all their hard work, especially this week when they had a live episode, and long may *Coronation Street* continue. With my thanks.

Mrs Margaret Graveney, Selsdon Vale, Surrey

We've had a bellyful of half-century hype, quizzes, countdowns, back-to-back screenings, screams, bangs, blood and gore, as well as incessant back-slapping by its own actors and fellow celebrities – even the bizarre inclusion of MBEs as the credits rolled – so perhaps it's time to commit *Coronation Street* to backstage for, say, six months.

Alternatively, ITV could launch an exclusive *Coronation Street* channel so those of us who dislike this hugely overrated soap can be spared its ubiquitous presence in the mainstream listings.

Graham Andrews, Bideford, Devon

I'm told that the ashes of the cat that used to appear in the introduction to *Coronation Street* have been sold at auction for around £800. Is this a case of 'Ash in the Attic'?

Joan Lock, Aylesford, Kent

Reality check

I feel sorry for *EastEnders* actress Samantha Womack having been called a murdering **** by a viewer while she was going about her normal life. It must have been particularly unpleasant for her as she was with her two children. No doubt the culprit also believes in Santa Claus.

Having had a couple of parts in *EastEnders* in the past, I can shatter Samantha's attacker's illusions. Albert Square is a plot in Elstree studios. The Vic isn't a real pub and its front door doesn't lead to the inside of a pub – that's in another studio.

The fronts of the houses have no backs and, horror of horrors, the stairs in Walford underground station lead to a brick wall. Why not spend an evening trying to find Walford on the London Underground map?

Ronnie doesn't exist. All the characters are actually actors who go back to their own real homes at night. Aside from getting a life, Samantha's abuser should send her an apology and a huge bunch of flowers.

Richard Sirot, Walmer, Kent

The awakening of the wink

Some light can be shone on the humiliating television quiz game before it even had a name or a clear format. From a Ceefax listing of daytime quiz shows, I opted to attend a national audition in nearby Manchester, only to receive a last-minute phone call begging me to make the long haul up to BBC Newcastle.

The unsuspecting contestants were led haphazardly through a set of questions and points for correct answers were accumulated on grubby bits of crumpled paper. At the end, a vote was taken as to who offered the strongest challenge to the other contestants, whereupon I was overwhelmingly chosen.

Later, I was sent a brief note by the researcher saying that, unfortunately, there had been a delay in the pilot shows being commissioned. Much later, I wrote to the researcher and then to executive producer David Young but received no reply from either because I'd noticed from a later episode that my audition was in the guise of *The Weakest Link*. I remarked that I'd incurred £42 travelling expenses but, in theme with the programme, received nothing.

William Corish, Standish, Wigan

Would someone please advise *The Weakest Link* contestants that one does not get questions wrong, one gets answers wrong.

J. Reed, Hartlepool

I look forward to the episode when all the contestants on *The Weakest Link* answer all their questions correctly and Anne Robinson, who seems to have every word she utters scripted but still mispronounces many, says to the camera: 'I am the weakest link, goodbye'.

Roy Edwards, Lyme Regis, Dorset

A matter of taste

People who produce TV programmes or write about the sixties always make it appear that it was all about The Beatles, but it was at least three or four years into the decade before they came along.

Many more discriminating people – who were not twelve to fifteen years old at that time – consider The Beatles were overrated and that there were many better songwriters and performers around at that time, including some proper originals.

The Beatles were very lucky. They were juvenile and silly but thought themselves even more wonderful than their fans did. The trips to India, John Lennon's antics with Yoko and the clothes they wore were – putting it mildly – the biggest laughs of that decade.

Paul McCartney appears to be still living in this world in which he believes his opinions matter as much as he imagined The Beatles' opinions mattered to anyone other than their fans.

John Evans, Wokingham, Berkshire

Pesky politics

Browned off

When the wind changed on the Icelandic volcano, Gordon Brown was all set to claim the credit and declare: 'No more Gloom and Dust'.

Kenneth Oswald, Jones, Wirral, Merseyside

I thought GB stood for Great Britain not Gor Blimey Gordon Brown's Gone Bust.

Peter Sparkes, Ramsgate, Kent

In London the other day, I couldn't help noticing that Islington High Street, spiritual home of New Labour, leads directly to Pentonville (Road).

Arthur Johnson, Hale Barns, Cheshire

Nick and Dave

My first act on learning that David Cameron had picked a Lib Dem to be in charge of energy and so-called 'climate change' was to order a portable generator.

John Phelan, Louth, Lincolnshire

I bet Dave had a horrendous Easter weekend, what with coping with Sam's morning sickness and cravings, writing speeches to get votes (without committing himself to anything too complicated), taking the kids to the park, nipping down to Witney to see to the vegetable garden, cooking the turkey lunch, playing with the kids, making them pancakes for tea, changing with Sam into the 'nice young couple' outfits to visit a pensioners' club or two, changing into the cool outfits to drop in somewhere where youths hang out (remembering to remind Sam to slip into the Estuary accent), then back home to read the bedtime stories and tuck the kids up in time for photos to get to the papers before their deadlines.

Phew – he'll have to think about getting help in the houses! What – he's already got some help? We didn't know that, it's never been mentioned and we've never seen them when the cameras have been in the kitchen. Ah well, so much for transparency and openness. Obviously he hasn't got to that chapter in the Rapid Results Public Relations course yet.

Geoff Harris, Warwick

If Nick Clegg and David Cameron think they can run the country using their BlackBerrys, why are we paying for the Houses of Parliament?

Mary Wiedman, Hemel Hempstead, Hertfordshire

The funniest comment I heard after Dave and Nick presented their first coalition speech together was this conversation between two DJs:

First DJ: You'd think they'd have learnt, wouldn't you, after last time? But no, they left the mikes on after Dave and Nick's speech.

Second DJ: Did they? I didn't hear that. What did they say, then?

First DJ: I've got the recording. I'll play it for you.

And he proceeded to play 'We're A Couple of Swells ...' Hilarious!

Joanne Chance, Chelmsford, Essex

Following the catastrophic defeat, Nick has abandoned the AV system. He now wants to introduce his Roman Numeral (LD only) system in which every X marked against a Lib Dem candidate's name counts as ten votes.

W. Chamberlain, Worthing, West Sussex

On the make

I'm a pensioner now so if they want me to do jury service I shall expect the same expenses that MPs claim – taxis to and from the court, lunch in a five star hotel restaurant and the facility to 'flip' my residence or stay in the hotel overnight, as suits my inclination.

That will do very nicely – and I may have a nice little nap while whatever goes on follows its course. Otherwise, don't disturb me.

Chris Newton, Hemel Hempstead, Hertfordshire

As a taxi driver, I reckon I earn £100 on a good day. I'd be delighted to take Stephen Byers anywhere he likes and be at his beck and call ... for £3,000.

Or perhaps I'll take next Saturday night off and hire him to drive me into town and back for a night out. But for his £3,000 fare, I'll expect him to wait while I get a kebab on the way home.

David Gethyn-Jones, Berkeley, Gloucestershire

Good ol' Ed

The roll-call for the Labour leadership was Miliband, Miliband, Burnham, Abbott and Balls – a bit like Trumpton Fire Brigade.

Lestor Haslam, Woodford Bridge, Essex

We may well criticise Ed Miliband for winning the leadership despite getting the lowest number of votes but it's an improvement on his predecessor who didn't get any.

Geoffrey Reed, London N1

If Ed Miliband is thinking of a new name for his party, may I suggest the 'Guardian Party' otherwise known as the 'Polly Toynbee Knows Best Party'?

Brian Christley, Abergele, Conwy

Monkey business

At what point in an MP's career is the nodding mechanism fitted in the back of the head and the CD player for 'hear hear' inserted where the brain used to be?

Robin Thompson, Amble

I see they're planning to produce genetically modified primates. Could they please produce a genetically modified prime minister who keeps his promises and tells the truth? On second thoughts, perhaps a monkey would do better.

Mrs J. P. Oseman, Gravesend, Kent

Trying to please the mob

If the Prime Minister talked about the Small State rather than the Big Society, everyone would understand and be right behind him.

Jeff Sheriff, Stafford

I must complain regarding the constant silly use of hands or 'body language' as it's called by politicians and media personalities. It's not what the hands say that matters – it's what comes from the lips.

These people remind me of penguins rushing to the sea or birds taking flight. Body language is overused. Too many communications companies are trying to convince their clients that body language is paramount to success, and are pocketing huge sums of money as a result.

One of the worst examples is David Cameron who does himself no favours by flailing his hands about. The result is negative. Say what you have to say without this stupid hand movement.

Gordon Frith, Caterham, Surrey

Dear (not cheap) Sirs,

Are there (not here) any New (not old) Labour (not Tory) politicians able (not unable) to (not from) speak without (not with) thinking that all (not some) people are (not are not) so stupid (not clever) that they have to have (not have not) the opposite (not the same) of each point spelled-out (not in) to (not from) them?

David Bourke, Rochester, Kent

Mrs Thatcher's reign was said to know the cost of every thing and the value of nothing. Tony Blair's is remembered for having a price for anything.

P. Thorndyke, Diss, Norfolk

Whither democracy?

Only about a third of the electorate pays council tax. Where is the democracy in allowing the two-thirds of non-taxpayers the voting rights to force the other third to pay more tax?

J. W. Reid, Okehampton, Devon

The claim that many Arabs 'think they have a superior system – the rule and power of tribal elders' – reminded me of an episode shortly before Rhodesia was handed over to Mugabe.

In a last-ditch attempt to forestall Mugabe, a moderate black man, Abel Muzorewa, was appointed to lead the country. A gathering of the tribal chiefs was called to inform them of what was happening and a white civil servant explained voting, constituencies, MPs and the whole panoply of democracy. When he'd finished, he asked if there were any questions or comments.

An elderly chief rose arthritically to his feet. 'This "democracy"', he said, 'is the most ridiculous nonsense I've ever heard – you don't ask children what their father should do.'

Bill Tomlinson, Guildford, Surrey

It was French aristocrat Alexis de Tocqueville who observed, back in the 1830s, in his book *Democracy In America*, that liberty and democracy will survive only until the politicians realise that they can bribe the people with their own money . . .

Mick Bolton, Seacroft, Leeds

Hurrumph . . . !

Several MPs have recently been convicted of crimes. In 1812, Sir Manasseh Masseh Lopes, MP for Barnstaple, was sent to prison for two years and fined £1,000 for bribery, having spent £3,000 in bribes to certain members of the electorate. (These days, the electorate would be delighted to be paid by their MP, rather than having money taken from them!)

William Smith O'Brien, Conservative MP for Ennis from 1812 to 1831 and for Limerick County from 1835 to 1848, was a Protestant who supported Catholic emancipation. He incited a national rebellion in 1848 and was sentenced to be hanged, drawn and quartered, although this was later commuted to transportation to Van Diemen's Land (now Tasmania).

Sheila Bell, Codford, Wiltshire

An extract from the prayer, asking for God's guidance, recited every morning in the House of Commons before the business of the day commences runs: 'May they (MPs) never lead the nation wrongly through love of power, desire to please, or unworthy ideals but, leaving aside all private interests and prejudices, keep in mind their responsibility to seek to improve the conditions of all mankind.'

If members' honesty and integrity were beyond reproach and in keeping with the spirit of the prayer, previous/existing rules were/are adequate. Those MPs in breach of the prayer's code of behaviour should be treated as common criminals; parliamentary privilege should not be an issue.

Mr G. Chawner, Walsall, West Midlands

Going back more than forty years, the House of Commons Sports and Social Club was a bit run-down and tatty but very much loved by the below stairs staff who made up its members. They had their 'jolly boys' outings to Margate', their Christmas parties and other events all paid for out of their own pockets.

A few years later, the annual membership fee was put up from half a crown to five bob (twenty-five pence). The joke at the time was that it was put up to keep the riffraff out. But there was no riffraff. Everyone had respect for each other and knew how to behave during their short respite.

Time went by and the people who matter decided that they wanted yet another watering hole, so the old place was tarted up – in came the soft furnishings and the chandeliers and out went the dartboard and the snooker table. Out went the overalls and in came the suits, the high heels and the MPs – and now the punch-ups.

As is often said among workers in the House, 'It wouldn't have happened in Les Butler's day'. Les was the resident district works officer back in the old days, sadly no longer with us. All the changes were made to make the place look 'classy' – pity about the riffraff.

Les Shaw, House of Commons (1968–1998), Sandhurst, Kent

If nurses require degrees because they will be making more high-level judgements, why doesn't that apply to MPs?

Ken Lee, Lightwater, Surrey

Ebenezer Elliott (1781–1849) denounced the Corn Laws by portraying the sufferings and miseries of the poor in popular verse:

Ye coop us up and tax our bread,
And wonder why we pine;
But ye are fat, and round and red,
And filled with tax-bought wine.

No change there, then, with the conduct of MPs over the years. The present crop of freeloaders and cheats are keeping up the tradition.

Dennis Adams, Bedford

Is there any company in the country that provides its workers with a subsidised bar, allowing them to drink during working time to the point of getting legless and unable to perform their work?

The House of Commons is one such place. Tea and coffee are the beverages available to the average worker and the Commons should bar the consumption of alcohol on its premises. Surely MPs can get through the day without resorting to alcohol.

The Government can't preach to the rest of the population about excessive drinking unless it sets an example in the first place.

Duncan Coulter, Fulwood, Lancashire

Not so green as they're . . .

Are people aware that the Government is wasting taxpayers' money by giving a grant of £5,000 towards the purchase of an electric car? These useless vehicles produce low CO_2 emissions, but use electricity mainly generated by burning fossil fuels. It follows that they are not green or environmentally friendly. They are expensive to buy, even if taking the grant into consideration, and they have a range of only 100 miles.

It will make environmental sense to buy an electric car only when most of our electricity is produced from nuclear energy and renewable sources – which is probably fifteen to twenty years away. If we don't buy these over-hyped vehicles, the manufacturers will stop making them.

Dr Keith Matthews, Morpeth, Northumberland

A television reporter recently made an experimental journey from London to Edinburgh by electric car. It took about six days at an average speed of six miles per hour, which demonstrates the main problem with the promotion of the electric car as a viable means of transport, other than for local use.

Manufacturers should develop a simple method of battery exchange whereby a discharged battery can be removed and replaced with a fresh one at a garage, the motorist paying just for a refill, like the bottled gas scheme. Cars could have a simply accessible battery compartment of one or more standard sizes and automatic battery connections incorporated therein.

Franchised garages could carry stocks of batteries and their charging facilities. This would cut the capital cost of charging posts and the wait of anything up to nine hours for a recharge. If long journeys were made practical in this way, the market would open up and likely sales would increase tremendously.

If no one has yet patented this idea, note that I thought of it first.

John Perrin, Worthing, West Sussex

While we all shivered in the cold, thousands of delegates, including forty-six from Britain, at the expense of their own taxpayers, descended on Mexico for yet another environmental shindig.

Some of the discussion was about 'encouraging' us to use public transport, which in reality involves making driving more difficult and condemning those who want to fly off on holiday, along with encouraging more 'green' stealth taxes. But how did all those delegates get there?

The only environmentally friendly way to cross the world's oceans is by sailing ship. How many did that? No doubt that bunch of hypocrites thought it was all right for them to fly there and be driven to and from airports because they are 'saving the planet'.

Anyway, I am just off to the local DIY store to pick up some flat-pack furniture, paint and wallpaper and take it on the bus home, just like my local MP would do.

Terry Hudson, Herne Bay, Kent

Politically what?

While mashing a *swede* to go with my *bubble-and-squeak*, I was listening to a *fairy* tale on the radio about a boy in a *Dutch cap* who stuck his *pinkie* in a *dyke*. Then came the news: *Spanish practices* at the TUC, *Top Gear* in *a Mexican stand-off* and Stephen Fry has *bombed* in Japan.

In the Middle East, there's the usual *pork-barrel politics* and a *jerry-built* hotel has to be shored up with *old four-by-two's*.

The newscaster sounded a bit *Flemish* (just a *frog in his throat*) as he talked about a *kiwi fruit* being rescued from a *kangaroo court* by a *chink in its armour*.

Browned off by all this, I decided to finish the *Turk's Head* around my *Yankee* screwdriver, then creep off *gingerly* to get a *Brazilian. Yellow? Moi?* Hold on! Who's that in the woodpile? Phew! It's Eskimo Nell – I could easily have offended someone just then!

Anthony Sutcliffe, Elmer Sands, West Sussex

I had a dream the other night: the country had been taken over by vegetarians and chaos reigned. Things had been okay while they were in the minority, the meat-eaters respected their beliefs, left them alone to get on with it and didn't interfere.

But I realised things were starting to go wrong when little Michael Lamb was sent home from school for writing 'OXO' in his exercise book. Michael explained that he'd only been playing noughts and crosses but his explanation didn't wash. In fact, from that day on noughts and crosses was banned in all schools.

Shortly after that, at a Midlands village fête, the vicar's wife was evicted from the village hall and later arrested. Wishing to examine the local produce on display, she'd asked if she could 'have a butcher's'. To avoid a prison sentence, she agreed to veggie awareness training at the local Leicestershire office in the village of Quorn.

Soon everyone spoke in whispers, no one daring to discipline the Veggies for fear of being accused of Vegism or being Vegiphobic. A couple of sports commentators were sacked after one said on air that a boxer would make mincemeat of his opponent and the other inadvertently accused a jockey of being chicken.

Things got steadily worse. An elderly gentleman with impaired hearing was in serious trouble for describing his condition as Mutt 'n' Jeff. Many familiar items were banned or had their names changed. Old Speckled Hen was no longer available in pubs, sausage dogs were ineligible at Crufts, Beefeaters became Beaneaters, Lambretta scooters were removed from the showrooms, the Liver Birds were hauled down and West Ham United FC was suspended from The Football League. Radio hams and utility meters weren't excluded. However, the Gravy Train was still very much in evidence but we were assured that it is now firmly under the control of *Brussels*.

I woke up in a cold sweat and realised I'd been dreaming. Or had I?

Steve Reed, Tamworth, Staffordshire

Objections to censorship of free speech are much too late. Back in the 1990s, I was doing contract computer engineering in West London and on several visits to Richmond Probation Service discovered that the staff were forbidden to use various phrases and words, one of which was 'blackboard'.

More recently, I was in a Starbucks coffee shop in Queen's Street, Cardiff, trying to order a normal coffee. I didn't quite understand what the assistant said and found out that Starbucks staff had been forbidden to use the word 'black' when describing a black coffee. Apparently the acceptable word is 'Americano'. I asked her what words were used when they described the colour black, 'Very, very dark brown perhaps?' A blank, embarrassed stare followed.

Spencer Brotherton, Bridgend, Mid Glamorgan

Further to the Romanians found to be living in a shed, I have a copy of the 1901 census. My grandparents were farmers and had a lot of children. At the end of the long list was: 'Edward Grundy, male, single, age 23. Imbecile (in shed). Does work on farm.'

No political correctness in those days.

Mrs Shirley Myerscough, Bolton, Lancashire

Reading that 'super headteacher' Dame Jean Else has been stripped of her title prompts me to ask: if this is the punishment for an offence that doesn't involve a criminal conviction, what can we expect if there is a criminal conviction? A beheading in the Tower?

Not if you're Jeffrey Archer or Charlie Brocket, it would appear. Perhaps the people who decide these matters are those who diagnosed Ernest Saunders with Alzheimer's.

Andrew Barr, Leeds

Political correctness means the death of the office joke? Ricky Gervais has already done that.

Bob Skinner, Felsted, Essex

Famous folk

Not a fan, then?

Why would anyone want to praise the lugubrious, physically stunted, sex enthusiast, grumpy, devious Queen Victoria? Many places in the empire were named after Victoria by pandering, grovelling politicians, while the poverty and squalor of child labour in Britain in Victorian times was among the most horrific in the world.

William Marshall, London E4

David Beckham is the epitome of today's footballer: arrogant, overpaid, overrated, preening, egotistical, semi-literate and – through sheer greed – destroying the game that most men love.

The likes of Beckham are doing to football what bankers have done to the economy. Real football fans recognise that Beckham isn't the great player he thinks he is. He's limited to one foot, can't tackle, dribble or head the ball and, on top of this, he's lazy.

Bob Bishop, Billingshurst, West Sussex

News that the Beckhams are sacking some of their staff reminded me of the joke doing the rounds a few years ago. Victoria: 'Have you seen the bottle opener, David?' David: 'Nah, I think it's his day off.'

Roger Vince, Upper Brynamman, Carmarthenshire

Victoria Wood says she knows what's funny? That's the biggest laugh I've had in ages.

C. Findlay, Newcastle upon Tyne

Jamie Oliver is reported to be worried about how his children will deal with his fame as they get older. If I were him, I'd be more concerned about how they'll cope with their silly names.

Ken Upton, Hove, East Sussex

Poor old Mohammed Al Fayed. He would have been better off slipping Tony's cronies a few bucks for the Dome rather than trying to butter up the Royal Family. We could have had red roses all up the front of Harrods.

P. Cooper, Hornchurch, Essex

Whatever salary Chris Moyles gets from the BBC, it's too much. He's a fat, overpaid egocentric who spouts nothing but drivel. How dare he compare himself to Terry Wogan?!

Ken Irwin, Manchester

Tony Blair's former spin doctor Alastair Campbell was asked by his local newspaper (the *Hampstead and Highgate Express*) if it was true that the BBC had asked him to appear on *Strictly Come Dancing*.

Indeed it had, the great man replied, on several occasions. However, he had turned the invitation down because 'it would affect my credibility'. I haven't laughed so much since Tony Blair informed the nation that he was 'a pretty straight kind of guy'!

Carole Tucker, Highgate, London

How long before our historically illiterate Prime Minister jets off to Germany to apologise for the bombing?

A. C. Jasper, Hadleigh, Essex

Notables

Pablo Picasso may have been 'the most evil man that Paul Johnson ever met' but he was without doubt a hugely talented artist who knew how to portray the devil, as witnessed by the drawing he produced in a matter of seconds on the bare wall of a flat at 21–22 Torrington Square, Bloomsbury, in 1950.

The flat was used by Professor of Physics J. D. Bernal FRS in an annex of Birkbeck College, which housed the crystallography laboratories. Bernal was a leading pioneer in the field of x-ray crystallography.

Of the wall sketch, after drawing both an angel and devil, Picasso is supposed to have said to Bernal (known as Sage): 'That's you on the right'.

Bernal had many other celebrity acquaintances, including singer Paul Robeson and actor Miles Malleson, with whom he had common political leanings. The story goes that English bit actor Malleson turned up at the flat late one cold night in November 1950 when Bernal was away, with a blonde in tow, and persuaded one of the students to let them in. Both my husband and I were fortunate to see the Picasso *in situ* in the late 1950s before the wall was removed and resited.

Hilda Palmer, Barnet, Hertfordshire

Explorer Wilfred Thesiger enjoyed a rich view of a world few now could imagine. He was fortunate to see the natural world before it was ruined by greed and the insane pursuit of the greatest of all illusions – progress.

Today, sadly, very few would venture into the remote areas of our planet without the back-up of modern technology. Thesiger said of the charming, serene Masai that they scorned everything the West has offered them – and how right they were.

He was able to see clearly what others were blind to – the impending chaos that is now afflicting the Western mindset.

David Harvey, Chippenham, Wiltshire

Quote of the year must be from the foreman of the miners rescued in Chile. After seeing his men all safely above ground, he emerged from the rescue capsule to say, most humbly: 'I hand over my shift.'

What a hero! What a shift! Those five words will remain with me always.

Nancy Marshall, Athens, Greece

Wondrous Widdecombe

Ann Widdecombe says: 'What really saddens me is that people don't care tuppence about what's going on in Westminster.' We might, if her ex-colleagues in Westminster cared more about what's going on in the country.

Michael Bacon, Farnham, Surrey

Last year the wife and I had the pleasure of seeing Katherine Jenkins, the singer, and Darcey Bussell, the dancer, in a show called *The Divas*. I wonder if we would derive similar enjoyment if a show was staged using the talents of Ann Widdecombe, the dancer, and singer Susan Boyle? Maybe they could call it *The Divans*.

Alan Cairns, Tadley, Hampshire

If we must be lumbered with ex-MPs providing television entertainment, I prefer watching Ann Widdecombe dance rather than John, sorry, Lard Prescott on *How To Look Good Naked*.

G. T. Griffiths, Mirfield, West Yorkshire

Glimpse of the stars

Further to the well-known stories about John and Julian Lennon, when John Lennon and Ringo Starr visited our antique shop in Weybridge they got to know my six-year-old daughter Lucy quite well and later began to greet her with 'Hello, Lucy in the sky with diamonds'. This was before the record of that name was released. Subsequently, John said that Julian had made a drink and called it 'Lucy in the Sky with Diamonds'.

The charming Cynthia Lennon frequently visited the jewellery section of the shop and a couple of times brought Julian, a very shy little boy who stood quietly holding his older school friend Lucy's hand while his mother tried on rings and things. So there was a 'Lucy and diamonds' connection and Julian had created a memorable song title.

L. Michaelson, London SW13

Peter O'Donnell who died in May 2010 was the creator of Modesty Blaise who appeared daily in a strip in the *London Evening Standard*, with her inseparable companion Willie Garvin. She escaped from deadly encounters with dastardly villains by wonderful ingenuity and her indomitable will. O'Donnell was inspired by the memory of a fierce refugee girl he came across in Iran during the war, whose rare smile could 'light up a village'.

The only reason she is not as well known as James Bond in my opinion is that the only film made of Modesty in the 1960s was truly awful. 'It makes my nose bleed just to think about it', said O'Donnell, who had little say about the production and withdrew any further film rights.

He also wrote a series of novels as Madeleine Brent and it required some ingenuity to keep his identity hidden – especially when he won the Romantic Novelists' Association Award in 1978.

Mike Fowle, Felixstowe, Suffolk

The man who has written the latest book (now made into a movie) about Marilyn Monroe is a dreamer. It wasn't him, it was me who lived very near the studios and climbed up the ladder she left just for me. Quite what her husband Arthur Miller was doing at the time, heaven only knows – particularly as they were supposed to be on their second honeymoon.

I'm told I was listed in her proposed memoirs, under 'great lovers'.

John Evans, Wokingham, Berkshire

It was an eye-opener to read of the £10,000 fee Fiona Phillips charges for her 'time'. Thirty odd years ago, my ex-wife ran a unit for the disabled in Chiswick, London, and, on its inauguration, actor Richard Briars was approached to open it.

He turned up on time, spent most of the afternoon there chatting amicably to all and sundry – and didn't charge a penny.

W. D. McClennon, Dartmouth, Devon

You're a card

The recent sell-off of five Pontin's holiday centres brought back some golden memories of happy times spent over the years. One such memory that stands out occurred when we were staying at Pakefield Holiday Centre in Suffolk, a few years ago.

My wife Maureen and I especially like the cabaret nights, watching visiting artists like singers, comedians and speciality acts. On one such evening, the cabaret starred a quite clever and amusing magician called 'Olly-Day' (geddit?). Olly requested a volunteer from the audience while walking towards my wife's table. Appearing in front of people is definitely not my wife's thing, but Olly persisted and eventually coaxed her onto the stage. You could see her shaking.

He asked Maureen to choose a card from the pack without showing him, remember what it was, then place it back into the pack. On the far side of the stage stood an Ali Baba wicker basket and after some 'magic words', a snake's head appeared with a card in its mouth.

Striding confidently forward, Olly took the card, faced Maureen and said, 'Is this your card?' Without a flicker of emotion, Maureen replied, 'I don't know.' The place fell apart. Olly quickly went through the whole procedure again and this time Maureen answered yes to great, if not ironic, applause.

Afterwards Olly came over to our table and graciously said it was the best reaction to his 'snake trick' he'd ever heard. He gave Maureen an autographed photograph.

Reg O'Donoghue, Walworth, London

If they had an Oscar for 'Extra of the Year', then I would be a serious candidate.

A film crew came to Eastbourne to film part of a remake of the classic Graham Greene novel *Brighton Rock*. Lots of locals attended auditions, and some of us movie-star extras were born.

The film stars Sam Riley, Andrea Riseborough (what a darling) and Helen Mirren, and we are all waiting to see ourselves on the big screen. They should at least invite us all to the London premiere, and I am sure that I won't be too busy that night. I am told that my movie-star looks are more akin to George Clueless than George Clooney, but because of my professionalism I gained the nickname 'One Shot Harry'.

A new career beckons for the miserable old devil in the background: 'If you'll just stand here, Mr . . . what's your name again?'

Harry Pope, Eastbourne, Sussex

Law enforcement

Never had it so good

It's suggested that a 1930s-style boarding-school regime in prison would be a deterrent for criminals: up at 6 a.m.; no heating; no radio or television; several hours of physical exercise; going everywhere 'at the double'; plain meagre rations (cornflakes on Sunday for a treat); a strict learning routine; fanatical emphasis on cleaning, polishing and general tidiness; and punishments (such as running with a rifle over your head) for failure in these areas.

A deterrent? No, this was life on the fee-paying Training Ship *Mercury* where boys from the age of fourteen were prepared for the Merchant and Royal Navy up to the late 1960s. And we were proud to be there.

David H. Wells, Eastbourne, East Sussex

Crime in the Isle of Man dropped by 14 per cent in a nine-month period when the prison went totally non-smoking. Even prison guards are banned from smoking and now it's Europe's one and only completely non-smoking prison.

Prisoners are told they have no choice but to give up and are given free nicotine patches and counselling sessions to help them.

Burglaries dropped by more than 35 per cent, assaults are down 25 per cent and car thefts by 7 per cent. The ban also deterred 11 per cent of domestic assaults and 8 per cent of vandalism. The threat works!

If criminals are more scared about giving up smoking than having a criminal record, why not introduce no smoking in all prisons and cut the 'low' level crime that plagues our society.

C. F. Beck, Sale, Manchester

In 1942, I served on a Royal Navy cruiser that escorted Russian convoys. A middle-aged Scotsman who had been called up as a conscript 'for the duration' was described on his papers as 'a poacher'. He had proved so much trouble in a small ship that he had been sent to our bigger ship but within a week he had punched the Petty Officer of the Cable Party, on leaving harbour.

To avoid a court martial, my captain exercised his full powers of punishment and sent him for ninety days to Barlinnie Prison in Glasgow, which had been handed over to the military as a detention centre during the war. It was the captain's habit to see all men returning from detention and when the poacher was brought before him the conversation went like this: 'Well, Able Seaman, have you learned anything from your punishment?' 'Yes Sir, it was warm and comfortable and they gave us porridge for breakfast.'

Geoffrey Prall, Sudbury, Suffolk

It's suggested that 'no one would deny that prisoners should be treated decently'. I would! Criminals should be treated with all the decency with which they themselves treated their victims, which is zero.

Prison should be the most dirty, disgusting, degrading experience known to man, not the pampering that criminals now experience.

Let's make prison an experience that no one would wish to repeat and, as a result, I'm sure we will see crime fall significantly.

Malcolm Roberts, Stotfold, Bedfordshire

As reported in the *Portsmouth Evening News* on 14 February 1913, a man who had been arrested in Newcastle was brought before the Portsmouth Magistrates' Court charged with abandoning his wife and child. He was sentenced to six weeks hard labour and ordered to pay the cost of maintaining his child in the Portsmouth union house. He was told by the magistrates that he was unworthy to be called a man or a father.

Now, less than a hundred years later, the moral fabric of our society has degraded to the extent that a man can abandon his family with no retribution from society whatsoever.

David Lee, Emsworth, Hampshire

If the 159th initiative on crime prevention doesn't work, the Home Secretary should go for the ultimate: waving of the forefinger and saying 'Naughty, Naughty!' – that should have them quaking in their trainers.

P. A. Maller, Weston-Super-Mare, Somerset

Beating up an old man with cancer isn't considered worthy of a spell in jail but copying one of Tracy Emin's so called artworks (ha, ha) to sell to some stupid punter gets a sixteen-month jail sentence.

No wonder 'law and order' in this country is considered by many to be a total farce.

Ron Holloway, Ruislip

Our governments always take the easy way out, which means whatever the problem and no matter how few the trouble-makers, we all must suffer. We saw it with the gun laws and now it's going to happen with the price of alcoholic drinks.

Our governments haven't the wit, or the guts, to solve society's problems. It's like being back at school where the whole class was kept back because of the wrongdoings of a few.

Phil Granger, West Malling, Kent

What does get you locked up these days? Try not paying your council tax.

Raymond Gallagher, Crowborough, East Sussex

A policeman's lot . . .

When I was a lad, my father told me that if I was afraid of something, I should go and find a policeman to help me. Now, I find myself telling my son to be afraid of policemen and not to approach them or speak to them. A sad sign of the times I'm sorry to say.

Steve Day, Stockton

Why were there only 225 policemen available to monitor the huge student protest? The answer's simple . . . all the others were in detention for not completing their personal risk assessment forms correctly.

T. G. Unsworth, Walton, Cheshire

As a retired police officer, I was amazed to read that a police inspector in Cambridgeshire had informed his local authority that his officers would no longer patrol a park area after 8 p.m. because they can't see. Do they all stay in the police station until it's light again in case the 'bogeyman' gets them?

I remember how during my first days at police training school a sergeant informed us that some of us may pay the ultimate sacrifice in 'the job'. We knew and accepted the risks when we joined but we wanted to serve.

Many of our patrols included dark areas without lighting or where street lighting was switched off at midnight. Areas included building sites, where – believe it or not – people often stole things after 8 p.m. and were arrested. Often, I sat in buildings at night in the dark waiting for burglars after information had been received about a possible burglary.

No one wants to see officers killed or injured but unfortunately there comes a time when, because of the very nature of the work, there's a possibility that it may happen. By its very nature, policing exposes people to danger.

If that Cambridge inspector or his officers can't see what's going on at night, there's a little gadget on the market which will help them – it's called a torch. If necessary, run a course to show them how to use a torch. Police officers are well paid nowadays. If they refuse to carry out their duties, including patrolling areas in the dark, they should resign and let others take over who will do it.

Norman Davies, Ebbw Vale, Monmouthshire

That German policeman who was granted extra holiday as compensation for time spent donning and doffing his uniform should have been directed towards an easier and more lucrative solution. He should have been given an evening job as a strippergram. Hen parties would cheerfully pay to watch him spending fifteen minutes taking off his police costume.

Francis Harvey, Bristol

David Cameron was right to complain about the Facebook pages eulogising Raoul Moat but this sort of thing is nothing new. Football thugs were goading the police with the 'Harry-Roberts-is-our-friend, he-kills-coppers' chant thirty years ago.

Ian Frewer, Colchester, Essex

Having admired the heroic day-to-day activities of Ian Martin who defused twelve bombs in one day, risking his life against the unstable bombs he made safe while in danger of being shot by snipers (all in a day's work), I then read about a pathetic incident in which a community support 'officer', called Clair North, was hit by a snowball and then feared for her safety. She was so traumatised that she's seeking compensation.

She's a perfect reason why these people are just wasting

public money. It would be interesting to know how much she's getting paid, compared with Ian Martin.

J. Michael Leather, Onchan, Isle of Man

Humberside police are informing shopkeepers not to phone 999 for thefts under £20. Kids stealing a daily Mars Bar are being encouraged to up their game and get with the program.

Alan Aitchison, Wakefield

How can the police expect us to believe their claims of understaffing when they can send fifty-nine armed cops to the Mark Saunders incident?

Philip North, Brigg, Lincolnshire

Was I the only one to notice the fleet of new police BMW estate cars pulling out of the station at the end of a TV item on the proposed funding cuts for the police?

Martin Heard, Greasby, Wirral

Our free-spending Chief Constable here in Devon has given us a marketing department, complete with a marketing manager, marketing officers, marketing assistants, et al.

Quite why a police force should need marketing is beyond me but what is certain is that these people neither prevent nor detect crime – which is what I thought a police force was for.

P. F. North, Exeter

My son and I were woken in the early hours by somebody breaking into my son's van, which was parked on our drive. We dressed quickly while my wife phoned the police.

My son chased two men down the road and I followed in our car but the time taken to dress gave them a head start and we lost them.

Our local police station is just down the road and my son's pursuit took him right past it – police cars outside, lights on, he could smell the coffee – and he thought his luck was in. He knocked on the door and a policeman answered to whom my son explained what was happening. 'Oh no,' the policeman said, 'we don't respond to knocks on the door. You must go and phone the 0800 number.'

What a complete waste of time.

Colin Matthews, Stonehouse, Gloucestershire

The latest reduction in the number of burglaries owes more to the persistence of double-glazing salesmen than to the efforts of the police or government.

L. T. Collis, Banstead, Surrey

If police must remove shoes, have no dogs and provide a prayer mat when raiding certain homes, the smart thing for suspects to do would be to spill a box of drawing pins.

Peter Hall, Marazion, Cornwall

In the early 1970s, a policeman by the name of Peter Slimon was walking along Kensington High Street one morning when he came across an armed bank raid at the NatWest at the junction with Campden Hill Road.

When he confronted the robbers, they pointed their guns at what they assumed to be an unarmed officer. However, he happened to be returning from his tour of duty guarding the nearby Russian Embassy and he was one of the few armed police officers on duty in London that day. He simply drew his police issue revolver and shot the robbers.

It's surely high time that a random selection of our police officers on each shift carried arms so that by the laws of average there would have been one around to confront Derrick Bird on that fateful day in Whitehaven when he shot dead a defenceless taxi driver.

John Kenny, Acle, Norfolk

All creatures – great or annoying?

Shot their fox . . . and other animals

Fox hunting should be permissible only to those huntsmen who can prove in the week before the hunt that they are, above all, good sports.

To qualify, they should agree to be dropped by parachute, with their pockets full of raw meat, into the centre of a safari park. On exit at the park gates, each fortunate sportsman would be supplied with the necessary 'entitlement to hunt' certificate. I'm sure even the most militant anti-hunt demonstrations would not raise any objections to this democratic suggestion.

Gordon Ross, York

Having lived in the middle of a 'game shoot' for thirty years, I'm increasingly nauseated and repelled by the abhorrent spectacle. This 'sport' is pure torture and barbarism.

The birds are bred and fed daily, taught to trust human beings and to be as tame as chickens. A bunch of sadistic boneheads then come out to the country and pay big money to mercilessly massacre these poor, terrified, gentle birds – and they're so unskilled that they rarely make a clean shot and each defenceless bird suffers.

We're repeatedly told about the poor farmers' plight but this is a disgusting, bloodthirsty way for them to subsidise themselves. Their argument is that if it wasn't for these shoots, game birds would be extinct – a poor excuse for their brutality.

If the roles were reversed and the birds had the guns, we would see the extent of the farmers' true grit. This is without doubt an outdated, barbaric and cruel activity which should surely be outlawed – it makes fox hunting look comparatively tame (at least the fox is a wild animal and has an inbred basic instinct to be aware of danger).

Joy Lucas, Thurlaston, Leicestershire

The late Tony Banks MP used to say we should be allowed to carry on feeding the pigeons in Trafalgar Square as 'they've been here since Roman times'. I was at the British Museum recently and photographed a beautiful Roman mosaic showing a dog hunting a wild boar – another activity carried out since Roman times.

How is it, then, that Mr Banks was so outspoken on the apparent 'barbarity' of hunting while using historical evidence as a defence for the pigeons?

Both activities are an intrinsic part of our culture and should be allowed to continue.

Janet Wood, Chelmer Village, Essex

If I and a group of friends went into town one afternoon and followed people just in case they shoplifted or committed an offence, we would be called 'vigilantes' and, I suspect, be given short shrift by all concerned.

But in the countryside, when I go out with friends to follow the hounds, we're harassed by people who call themselves 'hunt monitors' – but they are, in fact, nothing more than vigilantes themselves.

S. R. Jones, Dulverton, Somerset

The photograph of a fearful Camilla, inside the royal car caught amid the student riots, was not without its irony. Perhaps she might now better understand how it feels to be the target of a baying pack – as is the terrified wildlife when relentlessly pursued and cornered by her hunting associates.

John Rimington, Hare Preservation Trust, Leighton Buzzard, Bedfordshire

With the loss of a popular country pursuit, I propose an alternative. What about hanging a rabbit on a large hook, attached to a long line? When a fox tries to eat the rabbit, the hook will attach itself to the fox's mouth. I could then pull the fox from its natural environment and club it over the head.

Because this will be for 'sport', I shall then have a picture taken of the fox and myself to prove my 'skill' (though I'll be the only one smiling because the fox is unlikely to have much of a mouth left).

I propose to call this new activity 'foxing'. I wonder if it will catch on with the working classes?

Mr A. Kane, London

Now that the Government has banned hunting with horses and hounds because it thinks it cruel that a couple of dozen foxes may or may not be killed each year, it's emerged that domestic cats kill something in the region of 275,000,000 other small animals such as voles, sparrows, etc. every year.

Can we now expect a similar bill banning the ownership of cats?

Ian C. Beale, Kenilworth, Warwickshire

There has been much ado about foxes of late. We have foxes on our farm in Sussex as well as badgers and the way I deter them from our garden is that, like them, I mark out my patch.

If you collect male urine overnight and pour it around the area you want to protect, both types of animal will respect it. You will have done as they do and set out your patch.

I know that it works because badgers don't excavate my wife's lawn and foxes keep their distance. It's interesting to watch the animals approach the 'p' line and turn back. In the snow, it was well trodden on the other side as they about-turned.

This procedure has to be kept up so get used to drinking some good ale.

John F. Smith, Robertsbridge, East Sussex

Companionable creatures?

I understand exactly how Liz Jones feels about sleeping with her animals. Years ago I used to have excruciating migraines and would be in bed for two or three days. At the time we had cats and dogs. The peace of being surrounded by these sleeping animals soothed me far more than any pills.

Mrs P. Bunn, Horstead, Norwich

We used to have a cat who caught moles. We called him Crackers because in the autumn, when the leaves fell, he used to pick them up and try to put them back on the tree.

This year we adopted another characterful cat, TomTom. In the few months we've had him he's been shut in the shed and airing cupboard, and fallen from the top of our palm tree (where he was surrounded by birds, as if in Hitchcock's *The Birds*).

When my husband found a huge toad in the glasshouse, TomTom kept patting it to see if it moved, then tried to haul it around by one leg. Almost immediately, our poor cat started coughing and shaking his head while yards of frothy stuff drooled from his mouth.

In a panic, I rang the vet who said he'd never had a case like it, and if things didn't improve we should take him in. After a few minutes, however, the froth abated and, deciding that retreat was the better part of valour, TomTom went off for a lie down.

Apparently toads give off a noxious substance when attacked and the only things that can eat them without ill effect are grass snakes and hedgehogs.

Mrs Joyce Pearl, Boston, Lincolnshire

Good luck to the people who are going to choose 'house rabbits' as indoor pets. I had this idea years ago and the speed at which rabbits move and jump is unbelievable. I spent most of my time running from one electricity cable to another but most of them still ended up shredded.

And it didn't stop there! My rabbit managed to chew a big hole in the wall behind the kitchen cabinets. And as for being gentle pets – it often isn't so. Youngsters need to be taught to approach them carefully. A rabbit's back legs are incredibly strong and their teeth are sharp, so if they don't want to be held you'll know about it.

Ann Johnson, Runcorn, Cheshire

People have differing views on the seagull problem but I wonder if they would be so tolerant if, like me, they had suffered an injury from these birds. I was attacked with such severity that I lost my balance and ended up with a broken bone in my foot and torn ligaments, necessitating six weeks in plaster.

It's time we realised that aggressive and protective behaviour that is acceptable in the wild is unacceptable in residential areas.

Unfortunately, most local authorities are reluctant to tackle such an emotive issue. The gulls seem to have full protection from 'bunny hugging' societies who completely disregard the importance of people's health and safety.

Mrs M. E. Munro, Weymouth, Dorset

I'm a staunch supporter of the animal welfare group, Viva!, but can't agree with its founder, Juliet Gellatley, that the grey squirrel is a beautiful creature and shouldn't be killed and eaten. A non-native, sly, murderous little tree rat would be a more realistic description of this creature.

This imported American pest has all but eliminated our lovely native red squirrels and unless a nationwide cull of the grey is instigated, our native songbirds will continue to decline. They're easy prey for grey squirrels, which destroy their nests, eating both eggs and young. The RSPCA should not have prosecuted a bird lover for capturing and drowning a grey squirrel.

Nick Bali, Leigh-on-Sea, Essex

I'm horrified at reports that the latest 'must have' pet is a skunk. When will we ever learn?

Alien species, especially from a temperate zone, all too often have a devastating effect on native species. One only has to think of the American mink and the signal crayfish. If skunks are in this country in any numbers, inevitably some will escape or (horrible thought) be turned loose by sentimental people who are bored with them but unwilling to have them put down.

Once the genie of an alien species is out of the bottle, there's no putting it back, as the grey squirrel proved. I would vote for any political party that would introduce very tight restrictions on what animals are allowed into this country, either as pets or for commercial reasons.

Andrew Staines, London N22

Opinion or fact?

Get it right!

Why do so many people use the foolish and annoying catchphrase 'learning curve', demonstrating their ignorance of the meaning of the expression?

A learning curve is a graph of changes in performance standards, used to evaluate training methods or aptitudes. These days, we get frequent references to individuals or teams being 'on a learning curve' and, in an example I heard, a sports pundit spoke of a difficult learning process as 'a steep learning curve' – when a steep learning curve indicates that something is easy to learn.

John Blundell, Bolton

I enjoyed the Battle of Hastings edition of the *Daily Mail* but must take issue with the price at 'one groat'. A friend of mine who is President of Wessex Numismatic Society says no groats were minted in 1066; pennies were the currency, four of which would have been equivalent, eventually, to one groat.

The first groats were minted in small quantities under Edward I between 1272 and 1307. From the 1350s, the groat was then minted in large quantities for general circulation.

Elsie Pankhurst, Bournemouth, Dorset

I was excited and impressed by the description of ancient Norfolk Man. It's amazing how those with scientific insight can deduce from the 'treasure trove of flint tools and animal and plant remains' that Norfolk Man had 'a low forehead, heavy brows and possible cannibalistic tendencies' – despite the fact that any 'fossilised remains of Norfolk Man have yet to be unearthed'.

This truly is cutting-edge science and proves that scientists, when driven by almost-religious zeal for their world view, can make accurate affirmations of 'fact' based on their fertile imaginations, just as artists conjure up pictures of 'how the primitive humans of Happisburgh might have looked'.

They might equally have looked completely different, according to all the current data in my and the scientists' possession – i.e. none.

Graham A. Fisher, Buckingham

Advice and ideas

It's sad to hear of record shops struggling against the all-encompassing download market in music. But I believe this trend will turn as downloads are worthless.

Owning a CD of your top band is the ultimate pleasure in music and, of course, the collectors of the future will pay top money as these titles become rarer.

What could be better than owning Linkin Park's 'Live In Texas' album with the free DVD of the superb performance, recorded at the peak of their creativity? Also, the amazing Silverstein, AFI and Rage Against The Machine 'Live at the Grand Olympic'; The Offspring; Rise Against's 'Siren Song of the Counter Culture'; Hundred Reasons' 'Live at Freakscene', an incredible album; and the superb Capdown's 'Wind Up Toys' album, etc.

My advice to any real music fan is to get these albums now, or the top albums in their download listing, put them in a glass cabinet and gaze at them with huge pleasure as you listen to this amazing music. Give thanks for the huge talent and people who work hard behind the scenes to produce such classics. Recorded rock music has never been better.

John Barnard, Birmingham

We human beings aren't meant to be nocturnal; we don't see in the dark. If we lived a natural life, we would work during daylight, especially in the summer when our bodies feel like it, and sleep more during the winter months. What would be wrong with that?

If we fit solar panels on every building there should be enough energy to keep us warm and cook our meals. Wind turbines on every roof could pump ample seawater inland to be purified for use. I've always said we should work only four days, leaving one day for shopping and another for leisure, then Sunday as car free. With the roads empty except for emergency vehicles, people could go for walks, and ride bikes without fear of being run down.

If we simply stop rushing around all over the place in some kind of panic, as if there is no tomorrow, then we could and should ensure there is a tomorrow.

As for burying spent nuclear rods, what happens when there's a tsunami or an earthquake? The land actually moves way beyond the strength of any encasement we might construct.

Let's step back, give the world and ourselves a rest. What is money? Merely numbers on a piece of paper or on a computer. Like religion, it's man-made and has done us more harm than good. We don't need to work ourselves to death and even then be taxed, yet again. What a shambles we've created. So come on human beings, stop being so stupid and grow up.

Richard F. Grant, Burley, Hampshire

I've come to the conclusion that every prime minister should appoint a senior minister whose sole job would be to go through the Readers' Letters in each edition of the *Daily Mail* and put right, at whatever cost, all the injustices brought to light there.

Geoff Skellon, Abergele, Conwy

If MPs want to get rid of Speaker John Bercow, there's an easy way to do it. Just as he's making love to his wife to the chimes of Big Ben, order an ice-cream van to drive around Parliament Square with its chimes on.

Steve Gardner, Coleshill, Buckinghamshire

Perhaps the government's idea of giving iPhones to school children to spy on teachers' performances might catch on. The general public could be issued with iPhones to spy on prime ministers, government ministers and other politicians regarding such things as taxes, the NHS, policing, the crime rate, education, banking, etc.

Malcolm Tillett, Lowestoft, Suffolk

Speed cameras highlight the insidious practice of mixing law enforcement with revenue raising, which began in the early 1990s when parking offences were decriminalised. This country used to pride itself on having a justice system that was fair to all and the laws were enforced by police officers with common sense and discretion.

The government seems confused by the speed camera problem. This suggestion might help in formulating a policy acceptable to the vast majority of people:

Remove the monetary penalty associated with speed camera infringements, making the addition of points on a driving licence the only punishment. The allegations that speed cameras are 'cash cows' will cease.

Fund the cameras solely from the revenue raised from vehicle excise duty (the Road Fund Licence). This will ensure the cameras are installed at locations where they really will have a positive effect upon road safety.

A publicity campaign promoting the new, sensible and realistic policy towards speeding must make it clear that excess speed in built-up areas is unacceptable as it places innocent people at risk and 'speed in the wrong place' will be as anti-social as driving with excess alcohol and with having taken drugs.

Mike Rawson, Cheshunt, Hertfordshire

In the US, if a barman serves too much alcohol to a customer and that customer is subsequently involved in a road accident which harms someone else, the proprietor of the bar can face criminal and civil prosecution.

Is it too much to ask that internet providers should be held legally responsible when a paedophile gains access to children via their services?

A. M. Ward, Bexleyheath, Kent

Never mind garlic as an alternative to the morning-after pill. A humble aspirin – held firmly between the knees – is a most efficient contraceptive.

P. Kaye, Banstead, Surrey

I commend to the Government this comment by moralist Joseph Joubert (1754–1824): 'It is better to debate a question without resolving it than to resolve a question without debating it.'

This should be a guiding principle for any government and its constituent members.

Jeremy Parker, Henstridge, Somerset

Beyond bizarre

Melanie Phillips may be right when she suggests that the intelligence world sometimes plants false information about suspicious deaths of key operatives rather than compromise national security or identify any foreign powers involved.

During the 1980s this seemed to happen on a large scale. At least twenty-five highly qualified British specialists in computers and electronics died mysteriously in the Home Counties, and most of their work was related to electronic warfare, or was contracted out to the defence industry or GCHQ. The official line was these operatives were 'stressed out', and committed suicide, although most inquests led to an 'open verdict'.

The 'suicides' were extremely bizarre, involving clingfilm wrapped around heads, the wiring up of teeth to the mains, ropes tied to car exhausts, exploding vehicles and the like.

There was brief media interest in this at the time, but for some reason it never became a national controversy, and is never mentioned by conspiracy theorists.

Antony Milne, London SE2

It's odd that a married father of three should profess a 'Jedi' faith given that Jedi Knights are required to abstain from sex and relationships (a failing of which Darth Vader himself was guilty). It's even more remarkable that he should be 'unemployed', given that Jedi Knights have traditionally dedicated their lives to tireless public service. Could this be yet another case of a pious individual putting more effort into their attire than their actions?

It's also ironic that the 390,000 people who proudly identified themselves as 'Jedis' in the last census did so as some sort of inarticulate protest against conventional faiths when George Lucas himself concedes that his fictional religion was heavily influenced by legitimate ones such as Hinduism and even Christianity. It's impossible to profess a Jedi faith without inheriting the moral codes of many other major faiths.

Matthew James Dickie, Grimsby, Lincolnshire

There's an easy way in which our politicians can discourage binge drinking and free our streets of litter and staggering youths.

They should leave excise duty alone and introduce a swingeing tax on the packaging of beer, cider, lager, etc. The environmental savings on tins and bottles would be vast and thirsty folk would be encouraged to drink draught beer, etc., in their local pub.

This would help to preserve that most wonderful institution, the British pub, and educate a new generation of social drinkers.

As G. K. Chesterton warned us, 100 years ago:

God made the Wicked Grocer
As a mystery and a sign,
That men should shun those awful shops
And go to inns to dine.

Chas Wright, Uley, Gloucestershire

Scientists have discovered that each of us has a unique ear shape, which could be used to identify an individual at airport security, for recognition purposes, etc.

As a fan of 'the' Sherlock Holmes of the mid-1940s, I recall Basil Rathbone catching the heavily disguised spider woman (Gale Sondergaard) due to the uniqueness of the ear.

Conan Doyle was obviously aware of this a hundred years ago.

Derrick Jones, London NW3

Who knows?

I thought it a little odd to read about the investigation into the dead whale at Pegwell Bay, Kent, when only an hour earlier I'd read that an unexploded bomb had been detonated on the Goodwin Sands. Any connection?

Ted Wright, Herne Bay, Kent

Any shadowy ghost-like figure that appears in a photograph taken in Cornwall is probably not the Virgin Mary. In that part of the country, it's more likely to be a wrecker, waving her lamp to lure ships ashore.

Christine Bridson-Jones, Wareham, Dorset

Strange but true

Norman Tebbit was correct in his assertion that the V-Force crews were issued with eye-patches in case they had to drop a nuclear weapon. The patches weren't to protect us from radiation but to protect one eye from the blinding nuclear flash.

In the face of vast superiority, deterrence worked and was entirely credible. V-Force aircrews' life expectancy was rather better than that of the crews of British armoured recce vehicles on the Inner German Border had the Warsaw Pact started to roll westwards.

Wing Cmdr Handling Squadron John Whitney, Boscombe Down

When I worked for EMI as group purchasing manager, from 1972 to 1977, at their administration headquarters in Blyth Road, Hayes, an original painting of Nipper the dog, listening to the gramophone, was in one of the boardrooms.

In this case, however, the whole picture was visible, showing

Nipper and the gramophone standing on a coffin, along the side of which were the letters RIP. I was told that Nipper's 'Master' was lying inside the coffin and the dog was listening to his voice through the gramophone.

Keith R. Hall, London W5

Myth-busting

From Messrs Brackenbury, Ratcliffe and Lovell, solicitors acting for the heirs and family of R. Plantagenet:

We have been asked to act on behalf of the above with regard to the slanderous comments of 26 October 1485, asserting that our late client, Richard III, King of England, seized the throne of England unlawfully and murdered his nephews. Richard of York, one of the said nephews, is particularly anxious to refute this assertion, as he is alive and well and living in the Low Countries, and has every intention of returning to claim the throne from the evil usurper, Henry Tydr.

The Plantagenet family wishes to make it known that the late king was not in any way deformed and claimed the throne only at the behest of parliament. They wish to point out the many and great benefits received by the people of England before his untimely murder, including the establishment of the Court of Common Pleas, the institution of bail and many other acts designed to protect the people.

The Plantagenet family further make it known that they have received many expressions of condolence and horror at the recent events. The city of York has officially recorded that 'Our Good King Richard was piteously slain and murdered . . . to the grete heaviness of this city.'

We are aware that the press is under great intimidation from the tyrant Henry but feel that in the interests of a free and fair discussion these errors should be rectified – or we shall be obliged to sue in the sum of 1,000 groats, the proceeds to be contributed to the Fund for the Orphans of Bosworth.

Diana Lodge, Halberton, Devon

There is no historical evidence for the story we were taught in school that the Wars of the Roses were so called because the combatants wore white roses (Yorkists) and red (Lancastrians).

The myth was almost certainly a creation of Shakespeare's in *Henry VI Part I*, in the famous scene in Temple Gardens when Richard Plantagenet of York and the Lancastrian Duke of Somerset argue hotly. Richard plucks a white rose and calls on those who support him to do likewise, whereupon Somerset takes a red rose as his emblem.

Shakespeare's historical sources for the dynastic wars, Edward Hall (c. 1498–1547) and Ralph Holinshed (c. 1528–c. 1580), made no mention of roses being used as emblems by either side. The first known literary reference to the 'Wars of the Roses' occurs as late as 1829 in Sir Walter Scott's novel, *Anne of Geierstein*, though there had been reference in earlier centuries to phrases like 'the warring roses factions'. There is no evidence at all for the Temple Gardens scene – it was a dramatic device of the Bard's.

Roy Stockdill, Watford, Hertfordshire

It's a mistake to think that people in Christopher Columbus's day thought the Earth was flat and that if you went too far you might fall off the edge. This is a myth invented by a nineteenth-century American historian, presumably to make Columbus's achievement seem greater than it was.

The Babylonians knew the world was round 5,000 years ago. They, the ancient Egyptians, and later the Greeks, all calculated its size to a high degree of accuracy and this knowledge wasn't lost with the fall of the Roman Empire.

So why did Columbus have so much trouble raising sponsorship? The authorities knew pretty accurately how far it was eastwards to China and the Indies from the travels of such people as Marco Polo. It was simple then to calculate how far it was if you travelled west. But, in ignorance of any intervening landmass, everyone thought no ship of the time could sail that far without its crew running out of food and water.

Columbus's argument was that they had got it wrong. The world wasn't 25,000 miles in circumference but only 18,000 miles. If true, this would have placed Japan about where the American State of Nevada is today. Difficult, but not impossible.

Whether Columbus really believed this is hard to say but it was enough to persuade Queen Isabella. Despite this, he had to wait until she and King Ferdinand had cleared Spain of the Moors before she could spare the time to listen to him.

Fred Grisley, Barry, Glamorgan

I was angry to read that the Archbishop of Canterbury had 'apologised to a group of African tribal chiefs for the "inhuman treatment" their countries suffered during colonial rule'.

As a former British colonial myself and the daughter of two hardworking, kind, tolerant and humane British colonial servants, I think the Archbishop has got a cheek to make such remarks about something he knows nothing about. Several million Africans, who suffer daily under despotic leaders, will agree with me – and be puzzled as to why a leading churchman should show such ignorance of the good works his countrymen did.

The Archbishop's remarks do not help Africa one iota; if he and others of his ilk really want to help Africans they should do all they can towards reducing the terrifying population explosion there.

Gillian Trayner, Chichester, West Sussex

Note to fantasists, Tony Blair and Alastair Campbell: you were not the first to call Princess Diana, the 'People's Princess'. She was called that throughout the 1980s and 1990s, in newspaper headlines.

Fact. Easily looked up, I've seen it frequently. Also, called 'Princess of the People'. So sorry er . . . you guys. Headline writers can look it up easily, too.

Sally Kirkpatrick, Wells, Somerset

It was not unusual at the beginning of the twentieth century, before World War I, for children to be up before the Portsmouth Magistrates' Court court for playing football in the street. On one occasion, two children were fined for playing football in the street with a tennis ball. The actual crime then was 'Playing Football on the Highway'.

So it is a myth that playing football in the street has always been legal.

David Lee, Emsworth, Hampshire

It is claimed that under the 1980 Highways Act 'playing football on a highway to the annoyance of someone can warrant a fine'. I believe the Act actually makes it an offence for a person 'to play football or any other game to the annoyance of a user of the highway'.

In my experience, most complaints of this nature are made by people occupying properties adjacent to (not passing along) the highway and so, as they are not users of the highway, no offence has actually occurred.

For most highway users, any annoyance will only be temporary and they are unlikely to go to the trouble of reporting a problem. Consequently this section of the Highways Act rarely results in a successful prosecution, which is perhaps fortunate as it would mean that any child playing any game in the street could be liable to prosecution just because someone claims that they are being annoyed.

Neil McPherson, Gillingham, Kent

On men and women

What she wants

Given that Sigmund Freud said, 'The great question which I have never been able to answer is: what does a woman want?' what hope have we ordinary mortals got? For my own part, I think all a woman wants is a loving and faithful husband.

Derek Hanna, Newtownabbey, Northern Ireland

Can a man ever really tell what a woman is thinking? Nature produced humans by accident or design and biology arrived before psychology. Biologically, women want multiple positions with one partner, while men like any position with multiple partners. Psychologically, women have always wanted to change it, while men have learned to live with it.

The scientists will eventually design the perfect human, with both sets of mating facilities, and then we'll all think the same. Until that time arrives, women will always think men don't know what women want. But we do.

Richard H. Green, Wickford, Essex

The battle of the sexes

The constant portrayal of men as, at best, good for nothing and, at worst, seriously violent, illustrates the damage which the completely unnecessary so-called 'war of the sexes' continues to inflict on society in general and family life in particular.

After a visit to Bristol Airport, Liz Jones opines along the lines that 'all women are trendy dressers . . . all men are untidy tramps'. This is sexist nonsense that if presented from the opposite slant would be dumped forthwith.

Like most people in modern society, I've visited an airport or three, both here and in many foreign countries, and I find that as in most things men's and women's dress is good, bad, indifferent, or just plain awful in equal measure.

Has Ms Jones not observed the obesity, the ill-fitting clothes, the T-shirts with inane messages, the hairdos that look as though they're fresh from the jungle, the two-tone cleavages ranging from snowy white to sunburned red, the short skirts revealing unsightly thighs, the rolls of fat, etc., seen on some (and I stress *some*) female travellers? They are roughly equal in number to the blokish men who have no hair, sport several tattoos, wear singlets or football shirts, and have forgotten to shave, whom Ms Jones criticises.

She offers as an example of how to dress a geekish-looking guy wearing a formal jacket and casual shorts displaying bare legs covered by formal-looking shoes and no socks. I'm glad she's not my fashion guru . . . or my counsellor on sexism.

Dennis Shaw, Birmingham

Loose Women is a regular ITV programme in which a group of young ladies are handsomely paid to make, on air, sexist remarks about men. Sky Sports is a television channel whose two male presenters made, inadvertently and off air, sexist remarks about women – and lost their lucrative careers.

Equality?

Norman F. Smith, Oxford

Just when are poor delusional, egotistical, testosterone-filled male drivers going to grow up and acknowledge that woman drivers have been around for a long time now, are here to stay and are making a very good job of the task, equal to, if not better than, the majority of men?

The Top Ten list of men's complaints about woman drivers would be my Top Ten for male drivers, so let's call it quits, chaps, and admit that you can't be top at everything, bragging apart, that is.

Pamela Worsfold, Leigh-on-Sea, Essex

In defence of lady drivers: Moses wandered in the desert for forty years; a woman would have asked for directions.

J. J. Mullen, Whyteleafe, Surrey

Has anyone considered the possibility that young male drivers might have more accidents than young female drivers because they're forever gallantly swerving to avoid colliding with young female drivers who are bowling along obliviously down the middle of the High Street at fifty miles per hour while nonchalently attempting to apply their make-up by looking in the rear-view mirror?

Jim Price, Luton, Bedfordshire

We're told that women use 20,000 words a day while men use only 7,000. But how many different words?

Philip J. Cakebread, Banstead, Surrey

Why do men refer to 'the wife'? I've never heard a woman refer to 'the husband'.

Mrs C. J. Howe, Hove, Sussex

I totally agree that service staff demean women. What about all those waiters who address my husband as 'Sir' but when speaking to me call me 'love'? I hate it.

Yvonne Fryer, Sliema, Malta

I'm always amazed at claims of supposed 'sexual harassment' made by secretaries against employers. They seem a sure way of obtaining money for nothing.

I was a secretary many years ago and suffered unwanted gropings, and more, from employers in the workplace but a short, sharp, very loudly shouted threat soon put a stop to any further problems.

It began when I started work at around eighteen years of age and has certainly always been prevalent in the workplace according to many friends of my age. Cashing in on this fairly usual behaviour is just greedy.

Mrs Inga Sinigaglia, London W13

Risking a verbal pelting by irate women, may I put forward the suggestion that the decline in our educational standards matches the decrease in the number of male teachers in the classrooms?

At my school in the 1950s, music and geography were the only subjects taught by women. They were the most undisciplined classes in the school and as a result they were my worst subjects. I still can't draw a treble clef.

Let's get back to the authority of men in the classrooms.

Peter Hyde, Milford Haven, Pembrokeshire

We're told to forget Venus and Mars and that having differently constructed brains doesn't prevent men and women from thinking alike. But we know that those 'small' differences ensure that girls are precocious and take an early lead over boys – proof that the differences, no matter how small, affect the way in which boys and girls learn. We also know that women have feminine intuition and can multi-task better than men.

At university young men get more first-class degrees than the women in the final examinations. To conceal this proof that the sexes don't have identical mental abilities, the universities have now abandoned final examinations and use coursework to assess degrees, with a consequent increase in cheating (plagiarism).

The acid test will be when you regularly see women in dirty overalls maintaining cars. Until then you will know that men and women do not think alike.

Thomas Alridge, Taunton, Somerset

Professor Richard Lynn is merely stating the obvious: if the development of the modern world had been left to us women, we would still be living in caves. But those caves would be awfully cosy and pretty and we would all be vying with each other for the most up-to-date dyed skins our partners had thoughtfully provided.

The cave walls would have lovely pictures painted on them and, what's more, think of the wonderful make-up and fashion we would have invented for ourselves. There might still be war but it would be fought only with fingernails or flint knives, the latter again thoughtfully provided by our male partners.

Sadly, I fear Professor Lynn is right. Women are programmed to think inwardly and personally which, in a way, is lazy thinking. Men have a more outward vision that involves questioning the world around them.

Sheila Bell, Codford, Wiltshire

Jane Austen, with her intimate knowledge of human emotions, knew perfectly well how easily women are bowled over by a handsome, smiling face. Of course Elizabeth Bennet would have fallen for the charismatic Wickham; she wouldn't have been guilty or capable of the cold, rational judgement made by her impoverished father who could see in Wickham only the financial insecurity of being born a second son.

Austen's brilliant perception of human emotions is evident in her intuitive and accurate portrayal of these two literary characters. Henry James's Isabel Archer is, by contrast, inadequately drawn. James never gives the reader an insight into Isabel's personal feelings.

Incredibly, in a book of 628 pages, he fails to find room to include the pivotal period in his 'intelligent' heroine's life when she not only makes her flawed decision to marry the odious

Osmond but also suffers the loss of her young baby. James obviously shrank from including these two important episodes because he didn't feel sufficiently attuned to the complex human emotions experienced at such times to risk describing them. Emotionally, he was out of his depth. Jane Austen would have had no such difficulty.

Diana Townley, Cheam, London

Why should any woman who describes herself as very attractive be advertising for a partner on internet dating sites?

J. Pester, Wokingham

Figure work

Remember the old Atlantean double-decker buses? Their rear ends looked exactly like Miss Vorderman's.

Clive Coombes, Plymouth, Devon

How can there be equality when the richest woman in Europe – Katrin Radmacher – also has the nicest legs?

Brian Christley, Abergele, Conwy

May I just make a stand for the poor 'unfortunate' women who are a true size ten with no effort, either with regard to diet or exercise, etc. We actually do exist and our lives are generally made hell. We don't have to disguise our shapes or tailor clothes to fit and look good.

Nonetheless, we are *real* women in a way in which larger women who try to alter their shapes in one way or another are not.

Tessa Carpenter, Clophill, Beds.

What's the big deal about tall men? If the average British female adores looking her man straight in the eye, the ideal male height is five foot six inches. Napoleon was a pocket battleship and Josephine thought he was drop-dead gorgeous. Innumerable Hollywood stars are known for being short – James Cagney, Michael J. Fox, cowboy Alan Ladd (who preferred shorter horses), Dudley Moor and Danny De Vito (inside leg measurement twenty-one inches) – to name but a few.

Short can be beautiful. Take, for instance, insomniacal sleepwalker, crown Prince Leopold of Austria, who at four foot six inches was known to pace restlessly back and forth at night underneath his four-poster bed before making high decisions of state. And UK hotels magnate Sir Charles Forte frequently used the boy's urinal in the gents' toilet at the Savoy.

Geordie Campbell (five foot three inches), Woking, Surrey

As a six foot three inch male with a good physique but not the looks to match, and who has spent many years 'being tall' and always in a relationship with a female, I've found being tall is an advantage in attracting women physically – but doesn't have anything like the pulling power of money.

Being tall also has a down side. Having experienced more women than most shorter men, you soon realise that the

mystique of women is dispelled much more quickly with experience and discover that integrity is a rare thing on Venus –
ruthlessness seems to be second nature to them.

In short, being tall makes women look up to you – but you
end up looking down on them.

Barrington Dale, Thurning, Norfolk

Whatever the fashion

There's only one thing more revolting than a woman wearing
tights with sandals and that's a man wearing sandals with
calf-length white socks.

I don't wear tights anyway, I wear stockings. You can get
good quality fine sheer or shimmery stockings, although there
is far more choice in tights than stockings. You don't look like
Nora Batty if you choose flesh-coloured ones, and as long skirts
are the current statement no one is going to see your legs
anyway. As for black shoes with coloured tights, okay if you're
twenty . . .

Ann Langford, East Grinstead, West Sussex

I must add my voice of protest to what Jordan has done to her
daughter's hair. I was a natural curly blond as a child, so it was
the picture of Jordan's daughter, Princess, as she was that first
caught my eye.

My admiration turned to horror when I saw what had been
done to her hair. Why destroy a major component of her
natural beauty? To me, this is tantamount to mutilation, the
only consolation being that it is recoverable.

Jordan, please let your daughter have her curls back. There is no need for her to be moulded into a miniature you.

Paul Townsend, Cardiff

It has been suggested that the reduced sperm count in young men nowadays may be the result of the presence in the environment of oestrogen – this from widespread use of the Pill.

Could this also explain why young men, particularly footballers who have the necessary lucre, wear '£20,000 diamond earrings' that 'glitter prettily'? Also why their friends 'twitter with envy' at the sight of their 'emerald ear studs, the £40,000 diamond cross, the £45,000 Cartier watch and diamond bracelet'?

Such adornments, except, perhaps, the watch, would have been considered very suspect in my day.

Alan Charlton, Rochdale, Lancashire

We're told women over fifty shouldn't wear trousers. You would have to have been on another planet for the last decade to believe this. It's now rare to see any woman, irrespective of age or size, in a skirt, particularly in the winter.

Trousers are warm and practical and can look more elegant than a frumpy skirt. A smart trouser suit can make most women look slimmer and younger.

And what is it suggested a svelte older women should wear when going to the gym or jogging? A jewelled dressing gown?

Joan Riley, Manchester

If there's one thing a cross-dresser likes it's an even crosser dress designer. Step forward, John Galliano.

Vincent Hefter, Richmond, Surrey

Once again, a supposed fashion designer is criticising women for having natural curves. Most real women know he's actually trying to hide the fact that he has no real talent. His capability is limited to dressing people who resemble a plank of wood. This is obviously far easier than designing clothes to fit over bumps and dents.

There's a huge market out there waiting for talented designers to create clothing to suit the proper female form. But instead of designing for women, most designers seem to think that women should slim down to a more male form to flatter their designs. I'd love them to prove me wrong by getting off their lazy backsides to do some proper/challenging design work for a change. But don't hold your breath. I suspect most of them are incapable of it.

Christine Hills, Leicester

It's suggested that 'nude' has replaced 'flesh-coloured' as one of this season's colours. Neither word is meaningful now, with skins in this country showing all shades from pink to dark brown.

Michael Plumbe, Hastings, East Sussex

Yet again I have visited a major department store to discover that all the medium-sized gents' clothing has sold out leaving only small, large and extra-large. This is because the majority of English men are medium-sized and they have got there before me.

The shop still has the appearance of being fully stocked but in reality little is shifting and most of it will have to go in the sales.

Do our highly skilled retailers not realise that by stocking a larger proportion of the medium size, they would sell a great deal more? I try to raise this with shop assistants but am met by blank incomprehension. Can anyone explain this mystery for me?

Simon Rock, Coventry, West Midlands

Why are so many men sporting the cowlick hairstyle? They have a bit of hair stuck up on their foreheads like little hedgehogs. TV presenters, sportsmen and quiz hosts all look like scruffy idiots.

M. R. Manuel, Taunton, Somerset

Yes, men are becoming more vain, now even wearing 'man-scara' and 'manliner'. Our teenage daughters tell us there are snaking lines around the clubs and pubs as men queue up for the loos to check their hair and make-up in the mirrors. And they don't care that women hate it.

I feel sorry for young women today having to compete with their boyfriends' beauty regimes. I'm just glad I married a real man before they become totally extinct.

Louise James, London N1

Professional footballers in hairnets and mascara I can accept, but gloves and snoods? Never! Whatever next, overcoats and sou'westers? What a load of jessies.

Bernard Watts, Ulceby, Lincolnshire

The bare necessities?

Domestic matters

As householders could be fined up to £1,000 if they fail to comply with new complex rules on refuse sorting, could there be a reciprocal arrangement whereby councils are fined by householders £500 if their refuse is not collected on the designated collection day, increasing to £1,000 if not collected by the second day, with the fine doubling if not paid within fourteen days?

Charles Latham, Romford, Essex

Do the Swedes get their domestic fuel as well as their food from the Smor-gas-borg?

L. G. Shackleford, Bexley, Kent

Sales of cookers have fallen by 13.5 per cent over the past five years but the number of cookery programmes on television has increased by at least 100 per cent in the same period. It seems that we like watching others cooking but don't like doing it ourselves. Fantasy land!

R. H. Ashton, Blackwood, South Wales

Could there be a connection between the fact that bed bugs are on the increase and the fact that so few vacuum cleaners are being sold?

Paula Sherlock, Bruton, Somerset

We live in a topsy-turvy world. Cleaners these days interview customers, not the other way around. They say whether or not they will do certain jobs, like ironing, emptying the vacuum or putting washing on the line.

Each one has her own favourite brand of cleaning products. And most women I know tidy the house before the cleaner comes – much to their husbands' bewilderment.

Let's bring back home helps who did whatever needed to be done without complaining.

Isabella Rose, Peterborough, Cambridgeshire

People are using the Greek word 'doula' to mean a mother's helper, particularly in childbirth. No doubt they don't know that it actually means a female worker marginally higher than a slave and is used as a term of contempt. The nearest word in English is probably skivvy.

David Britton, Flyford Flavell, Worcestershire

Anyone else get a Bonsai tree for Christmas? I have just read the 'care instructions' – the giver must hate me.

Kathy Dix, High Wycombe, Buckinghamshire

A roof over one's head

Why am I not surprised to read that young people can get on the property ladder only if they have relatives prepared to donate money for a deposit?

The majority of today's youth have been brought up to expect to get everything they desire with little effort. What has happened to staying in and saving money for a deposit and starting at the bottom of the ladder with a small terrace house with minimal possessions that are paid for? I can assure you that they would better appreciate what they acquire.

The downside is that their social life would suffer – not so much binge drinking, no new cars or clothes, no fancy holidays and definitely no massive credit card bills. Now that's a thought.

Joan Turner, Great Houghton, South Yorkshire

In 1958, my father bought a three-bedroom semi in Cheam, Surrey, for £3,000. He earned £750 a year at the time and got a mortgage of £2,250.

Today, that house is worth £350,000 – 117 times as much. Someone in the same job as my father's today would have to be earning £87,500 to keep up with that rate of inflation but the same or a similar job today pays only £40,000 at most.

This is where the affordability has gone. Today's house prices make no sense and this is costing the country hugely. As the IMF has pointed out, it's one of the threats of a double dip recession – but if houses were correctly valued and reflected properly in mortgagers' balance sheets, they would be technically insolvent.

A bubble is a bubble. There must be some way to rebalance the sheets while ensuring the stringent evaluation of houses to be bought on new mortgages.

Bernard Otway, Reigate, Surrey

Safer than ever

Visiting Sandringham church, my wife and I were horrified to discover that about twenty gravestones in the churchyard had been either smashed or pushed over. Some of these graves are more than a hundred years old.

Suspecting vandalism, we went into the church and told the verger of our discovery. He told us that he had been obliged to do it under EU Health and Safety rules. Graves with loose – or even slightly loose – stones and crosses had to be knocked down.

He was trying to find the relatives of the buried people so that they could pay to have the graves rebuilt. He said that this is going to happen in all churchyards. We sincerely hope not. There is something very wrong somewhere.

Kenneth Bull, Royston, Hertfordshire

My local council is particularly zealous about displaying yellow danger signs on every electric support pole in this area. The signs are nine by eight inches, made of a very good quality plastic and are fixed about three metres from the ground. They depict a person being struck by a bent arrow in a black triangle with the word 'danger' below.

How much these signs cost each, plus the putting-up cost, is anybody's guess, but if this is another European directive and is in operation throughout the country the cost must run into millions.

Do we really need signs telling us the blindingly obvious? Before these signs were put up, I never saw anyone climbing these wooden poles, so why waste our money installing them?

Alan Runagall, Rayleigh, Essex

As part of the worldwide Rotary effort to celebrate Thanks For Life – a contribution towards eradicating polio throughout the world – our local Rotary Club (Ripley and Send) wished to plant 3,000 crocuses in the highway verge in Ripley. It was a relatively simple matter of the club members lifting the small area of turf, scattering the bulbs, replacing the turf and making sure it was properly flat so all would grow again properly.

Big mistake! We're now faced with having to do a Method Assessment and a Safety Assessment to go before the relevant committees at some unspecified time in the future for a decision which will be too late to get the planting done in time for the bulbs to grow.

The idea was for Rotary Clubs the world over to plant millions of crocuses on the same day but this was effectively scuppered by the dead, useless and interfering hand of bureaucracy, which has no discretion and no contribution to make towards the beauty that was on offer.

Luckily all was not lost as the village medical centre in Ripley allowed us to plant the bulbs there to bring some colour as a reminder of our worldwide efforts.

Roy Baker, Guildford, Surrey

Reports of a three-page 'hazard assesment form' remind me of a British Airways flight two years ago. It's never a good idea to fly with a cold or flu as this makes it difficult to equalise the pressure in the inner ear but I had to go. I'm a cabin crew member for a national airline, and when we encounter passengers with colds, we give them nose drops, which usually help.

Consequently, I asked the BA cabin crew if they had any nose drops. They didn't but produced a Vicks inhaler – not much good when your inner ear is infected. However, before I could have the inhaler I was presented with a four-page form to fill out to inform them of my entire medical history and a disclaimer so that I couldn't sue them if the inhaler caused me any harm.

Lois Clark, Stanwell, Middlesex

Having needed to visit the facilities of the 'super loo' in York city centre, for which you have to pay forty pence per visit, I was dismayed to find that, while the facilities were clean and sweet smelling, it was difficult to use due to the absence of a coat hook in the cubicle. None of the door furniture or fittings had any edges on which you could hang your coat.

Only a fool would put their coat on the floor in a public toilet so I had to hold my rolled up coat under my arm, with some difficulty.

On leaving, I asked the attendant why there were no coat hooks fitted and was told that it was the local council's opinion that coat hooks could be used by someone to commit suicide by hanging themselves! Is there a high incidence of hanging suicides in public toilets or is this an example of a health and safety officer justifying their position?

Andrew V. Barr, Leeds

How long before you need a permit to wash your car (EU Improper Use of Water Resources Commission), trim your hedge or mow the lawn (Destruction of Foliage Directive) or go up a ladder to clear the gutter or paint your house (Misuse of Semi-Vertical Elevation Equipment Regulations)?

Clearly these tasks will soon require not only a permit (at a suitable fee) but also the employment of an official council Semi-Vertical Elevation Equipment Stabilisation Officer to stand at the bottom of the ladder and at least one Semi-Vertical Elevation Equipment Accident Response Attendant on hand with the necessary medical paraphernalia, splints, bandages, x-ray machines, etc. (to be deployed after a thorough risk analysis).

Sue Smith, Coventry

Does a 'conference demountable unit from the management resource' contain a quaternary-based faucet and ablution in case the relevant staff are caught short and necessitate adherence to germicidal awareness?

Keith Howieson, Swinton, Manchester

Back in 1956, as a callow twelve-year-old, I went on my first scout camp in a big field somewhere in Oxfordshire. On arrival, we had to erect a five-berth tent and trek half a mile, through overgrown nettles which stung our short trousered legs, to fill two canvas bags with water from a standpipe, most of which we spilt on the way back.

At night, when we were supposed to be asleep, I was ridiculed mercilessly by two bigger, more experienced scouts, intent on spoiling my time there. But I rose above it, determined not to be bracketed with the lad from another patrol who got homesick and spent much of his time crying.

During that fortnight, I broke my glasses fighting with another boy over kindling for the fire and scuffed my knees red raw. When it was my turn to make the porridge, I burnt my hand removing the dixie can from the fire, having disregarded the instructions I'd been given. I incurred sixteen large blisters, which were dealt with by our Scout Master without a trip to hospital. I had to serve a punishment for my foolishness and spent the rest of the stay heavily bandaged.

When my mother met us at the station at the end of our camp, she said I looked like a wartime refugee – but I was too busy recounting what a wonderful time I'd had to listen.

These days, my experiences would have started an 'elf & safety' riot and my good time would have been ruined by them.

Mick Jones, Northfleet, Kent

Family matters

Regarding David Beckham's parents' hurt over his choice of godparents for Romeo, this sort of thing happens all the time once a son takes a wife. We have three sons, each of which lives near his partner's family, meaning we see less of them and of our grandchildren.

I keep reminding myself of the saying 'lose a son when he takes a wife but a daughter is a daughter for life'. Just thank God they keep happy and healthy and that their partners love them.

Ann Hartshorn, Exeter, Devon

Sickness in pregnancy was regarded by most women as 'one of those things'. Mine was not severe but very unpleasant. I was sick from the beginning of my first pregnancy in 1964, when I was expecting my first child.

My doctor, Dr Miller (a man) was sympathetic and prescribed some tablets, saying 'You'll soon be okay.' They worked, although I discovered later that they were a placebo.

In a subsequent pregnancy, in 1979, I had no sickness at all. In retrospect, I'm eternally grateful to my wise doctor all those years ago because he could have prescribed me Thalidomide, the drug normally used for pregnancy sickness at the time. Whenever I look at my eldest daughter and remember, it brings thanks to my heart.

Patricia Colman, London SE3

It's just been reported that grandmothers who wish to look after other people's children will have to take a training course. And we now hear that scientists have discovered that fresh air and daylight are good for babies.

My generation, who had babies in the 1950s, regularly put babies out in their prams in the garden and took them for walks. Eureka! The wheel has been invented again.

Christine Greer, Macclesfield

Paternity floodgates

Our children were born twenty-eight, twenty-three and twenty years ago, long before my husband could apply for paternity leave. Could he take it now? He would thoroughly enjoy six weeks' paid leave to spend with his offspring, even at this late stage.

Mrs V. P. Griffith, London SW6

Ten months' paternity leave for fathers? That'll open the floodgates for sperm donors.

Doug Humphreys, Croydon

Food pool

The idea of a 'food pool' supper club where neighbours take it in turns to cook meals for each other sounds great in theory, and it may work for some, but I'm not sure the logistics of cooking one meal for many different tastes is practical.

I find it almost impossible to find a recipe every member of my family of five agree they all like. Cooking for the neighbours and their kids sounds like my idea of hell.

Mrs Caroline Blithe, London W10

Regional delicacies like Bakewell tarts or Eccles cakes are not vaunted enough. My wife and I have only just discovered Eccles cakes. Delicious. Life (and our waistlines) will never be the same again.

Mr M. Andrews, Uckfield, Sussex

I'm a connoisseur of unusual sandwiches. When I was a teenager in the sixties, every Sunday my mum cooked roast lamb, roast potatoes, vegetables and gravy.

Every Monday lunchtime at work, out came my 'Sunday dinner sandwiches' – the leftovers of mashed-up lamb, potatoes, vegetables – all mixed up with gravy. My friends thought it was hilarious, but oh, it was yummy!

Anne Ayriss, Corringham, Essex

My first encounter with a 'barmi sarni' was in the mid-1960s when I first heard the sound of loud crunching in the office, which was very distracting for the rest of the staff.

'Who's making that terrible noise?' I asked and suddenly a hand came up holding what looked like a sandwich. 'Sorry everyone, I didn't realise my cornflakes and peanut butter mid-morning snack was so noisy. You see, I had no time to eat my breakfast so I put it between my two slices of Ryvita. Anyone care for a bite?' he said, smiling. There were no takers.

Kevin Haughton, Eastbourne, East Sussex

Given that chips cause cancer and that tomatoes prevent cancer, will a big plate of lovely greasy chips smothered in lashings of tomato ketchup cancel each other out?

Tony Anchors, Didcot, Oxfordshire

If you eat cloned meat, does it keep repeating on you?

Mrs Viney Hilton, Hereford

I laughed at the idea that people would pay good money for a Magic Gadget Strawberry Stem Plucker. Do folk in the big city not realise that these gadgets come free of charge on most children's soft drinks? And for a few pence more you can buy a packet of a hundred or so.

They're called 'straws'. Just take one and push it into the pointed bottom of a ripe strawberry. It won't hurt, I promise. No red strawberry has ever objected. Push gently and, with a little practice, or luck, the stem will come cleanly out.

Then leave the strawberry soaking in a little alcohol and melt some chocolate; drain the strawberry and dip it in the chocolate. It might not do a lot for the poor strawberry but, by golly, it will do you a lot of good!

Christine Hawe, Ardgay, Sutherland

Are you being served?

The campaign against self-service tills in supermarkets is most important. I have witnessed, daily, the importance of checkout assistants (real people) not only making a difference to the life of elderly shoppers but also the lonely, sick and depressed people in our community. In many cases, the exchanges are brief but in that exchange of human contact, a life may be saved.

The wonderful checkout staff at my local supermarket exemplify the meaning of service. Most of them contribute greatly to the well-being of their customers, who in many cases just need someone to talk to, someone to care.

Self-service machines have a place for those who want them but all retail outlets, especially supermarkets, must make it a duty to the community at large not to destroy human communication and to operate a friendly (human) service.

I can hardly believe that human service and contact could become a thing of the past, with most of the younger generation never knowing what it was like to be served or what it meant not to feel isolated.

Rosemary Nemeth, Taverham, Norfolk

When the first weigh-it-yourself scheme came to a local supermarket years ago, I was delighted by the fact that some things were so much cheaper. But when I got a pound bunch of grapes for twenty pence I realised that I was holding the bags as I weighed them. Could this be a snag in the latest supermarket innovation?

Mrs D. Frankish, Whitley Bay, North Tyneside

I can concur with those who find themselves disappointed with supermarkets' own brand products. I was given a sachet of tomato sauce to accompany a restaurant meal. Under 'Allergy Advice' it stated: 'May contain: nuts, peanuts, sesame seeds, mustard, celery, wheat, barley, fish, eggs, soybeans, milk, sulphites and cereals containing gluten'.

After sampling it, I felt a label should also have stated: 'May not contain: tomato sauce'.

Roger Vince, Upper Brynamman, Carmarthenshire

Far from being a new tradition, shopping on 25 December simply restores a tradition established in Victorian times – despite their greater religious zeal.

Scrooge would have had problems today buying his clerk's Christmas dinner – and many of us can remember a time, not too far in the past, when many services operated at a minimal level during all bank and religious holidays.

T. Rumble, Saffron Walden, Essex

Whatever the weather

After forecasting a spell of cold or freezing weather in the middle of winter, why do weather forecasters always say, 'But the good news is it's going to become milder'?

One Christmas and New Year we had some lovely winter weather, just as it should be, with some good snowfalls and plenty of ice and frost. Freezing cold mornings with frost on the grass and ice on the car is what winter is all about. It should be expected and welcomed. But for some reason the forecasters seem to think we much prefer wet, muggy weather when germs proliferate and everyone walks about coughing and sneezing.

One of the great pleasures of living in Britain is the changing pattern of the seasons and the great variety of weather they bring. We don't want mild weather in the middle of winter, so the forecasters should be saying something like: 'But the good news is that next week we can look forward to some real winter weather with snow covering most of the country.'

R. Miller, Bury, Lancashire

Just opened the fridge to see all my barbeque stuff looking sadly back at me. And there in the garden stands my brand-new barbeque covered in a big black bag. 'So where's the sunshine?' I ask myself.

The weathermen have got it wrong again. If David Cameron wants to save millions of pounds, he should sack the lot of them and invest in some seaweed and a couple of fir cones.

Sydney Vaughan, Birmingham

I spent my early years without ever using suncream, in fact suncream as we know it today appeared on the market only in 1965 when I was thirty-nine. Now eighty-three, I still have good skin with an all-over tan and never use suncream even though I'm an outdoors type.

I do, however, take care to adapt slowly to the sun as summer progresses or when on holiday, especially by avoiding the sun for a couple of hours either side of high noon. Once you have a good tan you have acquired nature's sunblock – free of charge. Admittedly, not everyone can do this. Different skin types will behave differently.

As to why we're told always to use suncream, perhaps this has something to do with it being promoted by a multi-billion pound industry.

L. Gabriels, Oldham

Is it just me or has anyone else noticed how friendly a gorgeous bout of sunny weather makes folk – the beaming smile and willingness to greet as you pass by?

It's true that smiles and laughter can create a feeling of goodwill and that all is right with the world, despite the constant grumbles about the mess we're in. If you have any doubts, just see a baby smile and you'll know.

Apparently we all need vitamin D from the sunshine, especially after a long cold winter, and it's responsible for creating that feel-good factor. And, apparently, smiling is good exercise – we use more muscles smiling than we do with many other physical functions. Twelve muscles are used to smile while only eleven are used to frown!

But really, who cares, so long as you still have the will to constantly stretch all those muscles.

Peter Carroll, Paignton, Devon

Use it or lose it

We have a pension crisis due to the fact that people are living longer and what do some mad scientists do? They try to find a way to enable us to live to be 140!

Geoff Chapman, West Camel, Somerset

Traditionally, only MPs, judges and company directors are allowed to work until they're gaga. I can't imagine pilots, firemen, policemen, engineers, construction workers, miners and many others, working through until they're seventy.

Phil Granger, West Malling, Kent

Bruce Forsyth is a good example of 'use it or lose it'. My dad took up running in his seventies and completed his third London Marathon when he was eighty-four years old.

He was running, sailing and horse riding in his eighties and narrowly missed taking part in a 'bungee jump' in New Zealand by a rare flash of common sense.

Sadly, my dad died last April, just two weeks short of his ninety-ninth birthday. The motto of the Hash House Harrier running group he belonged to was 'On on' and that was his motto for life.

Naomi Olley, Buntingford, Hertfordshire

The pickle sixty-six-year-old married Lord Triesman found himself in after being red carded as FA chairman, following his controversial and indiscreet World Cup bribery allegations to his muse, Melissa Jacobs, reminds me of the wise words of Lord Byron: 'Like measles, love is most dangerous when it comes late in life.'

How apt and prophetic. I suggest other ageing public figures and celebrities take note.

Jim Oldcorn, Great Harwood, Lancashire

Going out with a song

Born on the sunny side of a Welsh mountain on 26 November 1942, I'm probably the most average person in the universe – below average intelligence, above average common sense.

Every day, I generate precisely 12,367 thoughts. I'm a hopeless lover, a so-so driver, have a dodgy sense of humour but am rescued by a wacky sense of fun and a startling sense of instinct. Done a bit o' this, that and the other, but yet to decide what to be when I grow up.

At my funeral, Frank Sinatra will sing *It Was A Very Good*

Year – and I trust they will say I never let anyone down big time. Just delighted to be along for the ride.

Huw Beynon, Llandeilo, Carmarthenshire

The funeral trade, normally recession proof, is feeling the pinch. An undertaker in a Bognor Regis pub was overheard saying that in order to make a decent profit these days it was necessary to 'think outside the box'.

Geordie Campbell, Bognor Regis, West Sussex

Money matters

Bank on it

If the Institute of Directors is right and economic forecasting is a matter of feel and judgement, shouldn't they be subjected to the same regulations as fairground fortune-tellers, spiritualists, snake-oil salesmen and witch doctors?

Martin Clarke, Killingworth, North Tyneside

Is anyone else bemused and frustrated by the way our lives are now dominated by pin numbers, passwords, and ID codes, all designed to prove we are who we say we are?

In the not too distant past, if I wanted to speak to my bank, I picked up the phone, dialled the number (which was printed handily at the top of my bank statement) and was usually dealt with speedily and politely. I no longer know how to get through to my local branch.

Nowadays, to speak to anyone providing a service, such as my bank or phone company, to buy something on-line from, say eBay, or iTunes, or to simply order food from a supermarket, all depends on whether I get that pesky password correct.

In my house, we now have an A4 sheet covered from top to bottom with all the information we need to be accepted by whoever has answered our phone call, and after a thorough interrogation we may even be allowed to relay what it is we want to know or buy.

This now scruffy-looking sheet of paper is vitally important in the battle to keep our lives running smoothly. So what do we do with it? Hide it in a secure place from burglars, keep it handy because we're bound to need it almost every day or cut it in half to make life difficult for anyone who happens to come across it – then spend every session on the phone trying to piece it together? Heaven help us if we ever lose it as our lives will grind to a halt.

Mrs C. Fairhead, Leicester

If William Rees-Mogg thinks banking isn't a casino, he doesn't understand the world of 'finance' – it's all a casino. The stock market, futures and commodities market is one big gambling den and it's manipulated by a bunch of unscrupulous card sharks.

Philip Hinton, Bussière St Georges, France

Bankers' bonuses may be large compared with most people's incomes – and I'm not 100 per cent in favour of them – but it might help to consider what they spend them on.

They purchase expensive houses and renovate them, buy cars like Aston Martins, spend money in shops and restaurants, go on holidays, etc. All this provides work for workers who depend on people with money to spend.

I'm sure the people on the shop floor at Aston Martin are very grateful that someone can afford to buy the expensive cars they make. And the same goes for the employees in the shops and restaurants the bankers frequent.

Also, like other people, they have to pay tax – at 40 per cent – plus VAT of 20 per cent on most of the purchases they make. So a nice chunk of their bonus goes to HM Revenue which all helps to support the unemployed, NHS, etc.

I'm sure bankers, like anyone else with very high incomes, have no problem spending money. They don't just put it all in a savings account.

Richard Gayfer, Salthouse, Norfolk

Amid the furore concerning the remuneration of the banking 'fat cats', we're told, 'Most bank employees, especially those in branches, work under intolerable pressure, being targeted to obtain "sales leads" and to sell what are often inappropriate and overpriced financial products.'

Exactly. As I've always suspected, these lower-paid placemen/women are willing to dissemble and deceive the customers just so that they can hang on to their pointless jobs – it's not just the fat cats who are culpable in all this.

So forget those banking adverts in which they try to give the ludicrous impression that the smiling, friendly face behind the counter is acting in your best interests. And why are they wasting our money on these adverts? If they truly wanted to increase market share, it would only take one bank to offer realistic rates to the savers who outnumber borrowers by seven to one.

But of course, one bank will not do this. They're all in it together.

Tom Watson, Sheffield

Our two pence and one pence coins are invaluable when you live in a small village. The local newsagent, chemist and post office are delighted when you offer them and long may these coins continue to be a part of British currency. Each time a small coin is made defunct we are all made aware of rising inflation, which is very depressing.

However, could someone enlighten me as to where the most useful coins have gone, i.e. the two pound coin, the fifty pence piece and the ten pence coin? Is someone stockpiling them? I haven't seen one for months. Perhaps people who live in the sticks use their two pence and one pence coins instead and restore the status quo!

Katie Wheeler, Norfolk

A tight purse?

What's the difference between those treacherous men, John Stonehouse and Tony Blair? Stonehouse wanted to be become a millionaire and then prime minister. Tony Blair became prime minister and then a millionaire.

Jim Trueman, Emsworth, Hampshire

Did the MoD get its £22 light bulbs from Harry Enfield's *I Saw You Coming* shop?

Phil Granger, West Malling, Kent

Those who complain of their eight weeks' training for a war zone, culminating in firing only five rounds with a .303 rifle got a raw deal.

In the RAF, we had just six weeks' training but were blessed with not only the five rounds on a rifle but also fifteen rounds on a Bren gun, which amounted to not much more than blipping the trigger.

The sergeant at the rifle range bawled me out for firing seventeen rounds: 'That man there, d'you think the Air Ministry is made of money?'

Chris Hebbron, Gloucester

I read that a Russian millionaire has offered to buy the *Observer* for £1. I've just paid £2 for my copy but perhaps that included the *Guardian* as well.

Derek Trayler, Hornchurch, Essex

A tale of two towns, Exmouth in Devon and Adeje in Tenerife.

Last November, I went into Exmouth, bought petrol at £1.19 a litre, parked the car for £2 and went to a high street optician to get a replacement for one plastic nose pad which had fallen off the glasses I'd purchased there. For this I was charged £2.50. Then I went for a coffee – at £2 a cup.

In December, I went into Adeje to find an optician as the replaced nose pad had fallen off. I bought petrol at 79p a litre, parked the car at no charge, found an optician who replaced both nose pads and refused any payment. I then had a coffee for £1, including some toasties with cold turkey and stuffing.

Rip off Britain? You bet!

Roger Boud, Exmouth, Devon

I couldn't seem to get my head around some of these eye-watering numbers that are bandied about by politicians when speaking of the money we owe as a country. Then I worked out the following: if I owed £1m and was to pay it back at £1 per second, it would take me eleven-and-a-half days. If, however, I owed £1bn and was to pay it back at the same rate of £1 per second, it would take nearly thirty-two years.

And we owe how much?

Kevin Taylor, Newton by the Sea, Northumberland

The joys of metrication

Further to the 1897 Metric System Act, I have in my possession an early Victorian florin, which has on one side of it the lettering 'One florin – one tenth of a pound'. Presumably, the government was using some sort of metrication many years before the Act was passed.

Peter Jarvis, Worthing, West Sussex

A handy quip says 'we should go metric completely – every inch of the way'. Our formal policy of metrication began in 1965, and in 1971 we adopted a decimal currency but the mandatory use of metric for packaging goods came only in 1995.

Though we're not wholly metric, the system we now use is the SI (System International) developed in 1960 and taught in our schools for the last forty years. It's the MKS (metre/kilogram/second) system rather than the CGS (centimetre/gram/second) system but, in practice, it often appears to be a mixture.

A more comprehensive global use – especially for example in

manufacturing – would be an advantage but the most notable exception to the change is in the USA, due I believe to the manufacturing industry's unwillingness.

Working in a technical college in the early 1970s, I had the doubtful pleasure of initiating some of the changes and now recall some amusing events. One colleague went to buy some timber. After asking for a piece 4 in by 2 in, 'Ah!' exclaimed the assistant. 'We've gone metric: that's now 100 mm by 50 mm.' 'And how much is it?' my friend inquired. 'Ten pence a foot', came the reply.

One lecturer ended his Change To Metric exposition with: 'We must now eat, drink and sleep metric – that must be our yardstick for the future'.

Mervyn Williams, Huddersfield

Let's talk about tax

Why is it that computer games manufacturers can produce thousands of faultless programs but the tax office can't find one that does simple arithmetic?

Fred Turton, Sellindge, Kent

A local income tax might appear attractive but I have yet to see a definition of it – and its success or (more likely) failure depends on a watertight legal definition.

Is it to be 'a tax levied, collected and spent locally'? If so, consider the case of Mr Z: he lives in local authority area A and works in local authority area B but his employer is a multinational organisation with stores in most towns and cities, so his earnings are dealt with at head office in local authority area C. Where does the tax deducted in area C go, to A or B?

There are dozens of variations on this theme, even down to one- or two-man businesses. Huge databases will be needed and have to be constantly updated as people move house and/or jobs.

Alternatively, perhaps the intention is to pass all locally collected tax to a central government agency for redistribution to local authorities, in which case he who pays the piper calls the tune and the agency would no doubt attach many conditions and the 'local' aspect would be lost.

The original rating system, until replaced by the toothless Community Charge, was cheap and efficient. People move, property doesn't.

Malcolm Astley, Wolverhampton

Five tax-exile peers left the House of Lords because of their non-dom status. And what did we get in exchange, exiled from his principles? Non compus Prescott.

Donald Coleman, Eynsham, Oxfordshire

I trust that the Inland Revenue is putting as much effort into collecting the tax from Rooney's hooker as they are in collecting the tax caused by its own mistake, or are these hookers exempt from paying tax on their earnings?

Mike Cox, Marlborough, Wiltshire

We've been aware of problems at the tax office for some time. Between 12 April and 29 April 2010, my husband received fifteen different tax codes in separate envelopes, eight of which were delivered on the same day. Could this be a record?

Shena McIntyre, Belfast

All things medical

Hospital matters

My cat fell ill at roughly the same time as my mum. For my cat nothing was too much trouble: blood tests came back the next day, x-rays, operations, etc., were all done as and when necessary.

My mum's initial blood test took ten days and indicated that she had cancer. A scan was arranged but there was a twelve-week waiting list. Before the scan she took a turn for the worse and was taken to A&E where she waited for four hours on a trolley. In due course, she was admitted to hospital where she finally had her scan.

Unlike our friendly vet, the NHS is a public utility, a bit like road sweeping or drain clearance. For an eighty-one-year-old woman, chemotherapy isn't considered cost effective. As if cancer wasn't enough, I went in one evening to find my mother covered in bruises. She had fallen from her perch three feet in the air (Health & Safety) with no side bars (Human Rights Act) to the floor. As usual, dry caked food was uneaten by her bed. 'We can't force-feed her,' I was told.

Using a little bit of encouragement, I managed to get her to eat. For most of the time, I was the only one providing her with food and drink. Labelled a 'bed blocker' she was moved to a nursing home where she received far better treatment but at great expense to me.

Sadly, both my cat and my mother died. My cat after the very best treatment – all of which was affordable – died from an overdose of barbiturates. My mother died from an overdose of morphine. It's called involuntary euthanasia and I understand that it's quite common.

I wanted the same treatment for my mum as we take for granted for our pets. I felt I was swimming through treacle.

G. R. Holwill, Exeter, Devon

I attended my local A&E as I'd broken my ankle while playing golf. They did a very good job and plastered up my leg and gave me some crutches.

I was given two information cards concerning care of the plaster and use of the crutches. On the back of each card was an advert from a law firm offering no-win-no-fee services to obtain cash from somebody. Is it the correct function of the NHS to encourage this kind of 'ambulance chasing'?

Tony Fitt, Fareham, Hampshire

If cleanliness is next to godliness, NHS hospitals must be maintained by atheists.

Tommy Gardner, Cowes, Isle of Wight

The NHS in Doncaster is piloting a scheme that provides free ice lollies to staff in their workplace. It's said that this will reduce employees' stress and reduce the large bill for work-related stress sickness. The £2,000 scheme is funded by National Lottery money – and more is promised if it's successful.

The day after hearing about this I went into work – for the NHS – to be greeted by the news that our staffing levels, already being reduced by 25 per cent while covering the same service, will now be looked at again with a view to further cuts.

I can only despair at the NHS and its way of thinking.

D. Brown, Doncaster, South Yorkshire

Hospitals have never been in meaningful competition with each other any more than the various branches of the armed forces are in competition over defeating a common enemy. Petty rivalries may exist but what motivates medical staff is the wish to provide a high-quality service within allocated resources.

Hospital staff frustration lies in the absurd waste of money in over-staffing, with too many managers, public relations people and bean-counters appointed to pursue the 'internal market' – in which hospitals compete with each other and earn money by the number of patients they treat (not how *well*) and by focusing on arbitrary targets.

Dr Barrie Smith, Erdington, Birmingham

So each time a patient suffers the indignity of a mixed-sex ward the hospital is to be fined £250 – thereby ensuring some other patient receives poorer treatment to the tune of £250. Brilliant!

Brian Cooper, Bushey, Hertfordshire

Medical burnout

My wife and I have heeded the many medically inspired programmes on TV and radio and items in the press to such an extent that we are fast becoming hypochondriacs.

To escape from it all, we like to spend a couple of weeks at the McBurney's Point Hotel on the Islets of Langerhans then down to the Med for a stay on the island of Lansoprazale where we will dine at the Ptomaine Restaurant and Polio Grill where Salmonella puts on exotic floor shows and we can dance the streptococci to Gippy Tum Tum and his orchestra.

Hadyn Murray Dodd, Dronfield

It pays to keep close track of your medical records. I admit to sometimes having trouble keeping my trousers up but I never realised it was a medical condition. Twelve years ago, I went to the Centre for ME and Chronic Fatigue Syndrome in Essex where the consultant diagnosed me as suffering from 'burn-out syndrome'. By the time this was scanned into my GPs computer system, it had become 'bum-out syndrome'!

Happily, my GP believed my plea that I have never worked on a building site and so corrected the diagnosis.

Phil Musk, Godalming, Surrey

The sad fact about cosmetic surgery is that, apparently, you either look as if you need it or look as if you've had it.

Rod Danton, Saffron Walden, Essex

No smoke without . . .

One reason why people continue to indulge in the smoking habit is because cigarettes are so portable. A packet of twenty fags sits neatly in the pocket or handbag. We require cigarette manufacturers by law to pack a larger number of cigarettes in bigger triangular cartons (similar to milk cartons).

Each purchase would become an investment. Cigarette dispensing machines would become obsolete. Shops would find it difficult to stock or display triangular packs on shelves. Discrete smokers would find it difficult to conceal triangular cartons in their homes, glove compartments or office drawers. Sales of cigarette cases may initially go up but a certain number of people would give up smoking rather than carry these unwieldy packs around with them.

I'm a lapsed (!) smoker but my COPD and cardiac profile bear eloquent testimony to my years of inhalation.

Ameer Janmohamed, London SW15

It's staggering beyond belief that some self-righteous person has taken it upon him or herself to alter history by airbrushing out Winston Churchill's cigar from his photograph. I recall that Brunel suffered the same fate a while ago at the hands of a publishing group who removed his cigar from that most iconic photograph of him standing by the launch chains of the *Great Eastern*.

Don't these people realise that smoking was probably one of the only pleasures to relieve these two great Englishmen of the huge amounts of stress they must have suffered daily?

In Churchill's case, there are still many alive from the war years and a huge number of us baby boomers who recall him so well, who I doubt have ever seen an image of him minus the famous accessory.

I would like to say to whoever is responsible for this, no matter what your views or beliefs, you have no right to alter history. Both Churchill and Brunel smoked and you and your modern retouching techniques have no right to tamper with their past. Save your zealous campaigning for the current world – if you must.

By the way, I'm a non-smoker.

Dave Baseley, Great Hormead, Hertforshire

We're advised that smoking, drinking and eating heavy meals in the late evening are bad for us.

In the early 1930s, when he was writing his definitive biography of the Duke of Marlborough, Winston Churchill would wake at 7 a.m. and study all the newspapers. Breakfast was at 8 a.m., with a menu that often included beef. Then came the work on Marlborough until lunch at 1.15 p.m.

Lunch was accompanied by champagne and followed by port, brandy and a cigar. At 3 or 4 p.m. he resumed work until tea at 5 p.m., which was improved by a whisky and soda.

Further work was done until dinner at 8.15 p.m. Dinner, with more champagne, port, brandy and cigars, lasted until 10 or 11 p.m., at which time he retired for more dictating, plus whiskies and soda, until 2 or 3 o'clock in the morning.

A few years later he became one of the most important prime ministers in our country's history.

Audrey Boyle, Halesowen, Worcestershire

Who cares?

We're told that people on a limited budget can't eat healthily. I listen in disbelief to women bleating on about how they have to feed their families 'rubbish' food as it's all they can afford. This is nonsense.

I'm a mother of seven, with five children still at home and we're on a very limited budget. My supermarket trolley is full of rice, pasta, potatoes, vegetables and fruit and the plainest of biscuits, cheapest of eggs and long-life milk.

We can't afford processed meals, chocolate, fast food, sugary drinks, endless crisps or full-fat food. If you're truly hard up, you have to cook from scratch.

Our eldest son is at university where he and his friends are on a very tight budget. What do they live on? Rice, jacket potatoes, beans, chicken and fish. The ridiculous excuse of the fatties is really wearing thin. Sometimes, when I glance at a fat person's trolley and see all the chocolate and yummy-looking things I wish I could afford to get fat.

Mrs E. Beall, St Leonards-on-Sea, Sussex

There has been a loss of communication when we're told that the National Health Service supplies care from the cradle to the grave. Many don't seem to realise that at some time during their lives they have to leave the cradle.

Katharine Sumner, Boston, Lincolnshire

The British Medical Association has weighed in on the Prime Minister David Cameron's health care proposals:

The Allergists voted to scratch it, but the Dermatologists advised not to make any rash moves.

The Gastroenterologists had a sort of a gut feeling about it, but the Neurologists thought the Administration had a lot of nerve.

The Obstetricians felt they were all labouring under a misconception, while the Ophthalmologists considered the idea short-sighted.

Pathologists yelled, 'Over my dead body!' while the Paediatricians said, 'Oh, grow up!'

The Psychiatrists thought the whole idea was madness and the Radiologists could see right through it.

The Surgeons decided to wash their hands of the whole thing and the ENT specialists wouldn't hear of it.

The Plastic Surgeons said, 'This puts a whole new face on the matter', while the Podiatrists thought it was a step forward.

The Urologists were p . . . d off at the whole idea but the Anaesthetists thought the scheme was a gas.

Finally the Cardiologists didn't have the heart to say no.

J. Fletcher, Coleby, Lincolnshire

First we're told that eating two rashers of bacon or one sausage a day could raise the risk of heart disease by nearly 50 per cent. Then we see the good old British fry-up described as 'the healthiest breakfast of all'. No wonder we're confused by the conflicting advice offered.

Until a couple of months ago, eating more than two eggs a day carried a sentence of early death. Now, apparently, we can eat eggs safely every day. Which is correct?

Bob Conway, Pulborough, Sussex

Rather than emailing your symptoms to your GP, why not cut out the expensive middleman and simply log into his computer to find your own cure?

If medicine is to become DIY, no doubt B&Q can be prevailed on to open a medicine aisle.

Ray Lyman, St Neots

My wife uses a wheelchair and we have vowed never to go to Ikea again. Their architect should be condemned to spend a week in a wheelchair.

Merrik Burrell, Malaga, Spain

Miracle cures?

My uncle farmed during the foot-and-mouth crisis in 1967. He had onions on shelves in the shippon (cow shed). It was strange that his cows didn't get the condition, while neighbouring farms did.

As onions are a disinfectant they probably prevented the herd from becoming infected. Garlic and onions are known for their disinfection properties and perhaps should be used more.

Mrs J. A. Colson-Osborne, Alfreton, Derbyshire

My mother told me that about sixty years ago my father was ill with shellfish poisoning. His hands were swollen, his face had changed colour and he was developing a rash. The doctor put an onion under each armpit. The onions turned coal-black and the swelling went down and he recovered.

I've often used onions on ant bites and wasp stings and once swallowed chopped onion with some mustard to cure a very stubborn sore throat. The doctors were amazed.

Vivienne Aldhouse, Aylesbury, Buckinghamshire

Okay, sport . . .

It's just a game

When I was a boy, back in the 1930s, I had a set of cigarette cards showing you various aspects of how to play football. Two of them I remember clearly: the shoulder charge and the sliding tackle. We did these and sometimes they came off and sometimes they didn't. So we carried on with the game.

If these cards were issued today, there would have to be a series of follow-up cards. In either case, we would see the loser writhing on the grass waiting for the air ambulance, half his team mates squaring up to the other side and the others mobbing the referee, screaming at him and demanding action.

A couple of minutes later, the game carries on. What progress the game has made . . .

Sid Stainer, Birchington, Kent

'Hi guys, welcome to the England World Cup victory parade from Trafalgar Square, with your presenters Myleene Klass and Emma Crosby. We're just in time for viewers to see, in the first open-top bus, Sir John Terry, Sir Steven Gerrard and Robert Green OBE, with honorary knights David Beckham and Fabio Capello.

'After them, it looks like the media buses, it could be five buses for the BBC, yes, and there's A. Hansen, A. Shearer and M. Lawrenson all sporting their CBEs for having given up crucial time on the golf course.'

'Sir, please wake up! You're having a nightmare, take these tablets three times a day, every four hours, these are very calming.'

Colin Park, Little Sutton, Cheshire

As celebrities rule the world, for the next World Cup we must produce a celebrity team. Here's my suggestion:

Manager: Al Murray the Pub Landlord (self explanatory).
Coach: Mr Motivator (self explanatory)

Goalkeeper: Elton John (sequins dazzle the opposition). Defenders: Matt Lucas as Bubbles De Vere (hard to get around); Robbie Williams (Take That ball every time); Keith Allen (as the Sheriff of Nottingham, a mean defender); Ewan McGregor (great actor, fools the ref)

Midfield: Prof Brian Cox (drop-dead looks tranfixes the opposition); Wallace (& Gromit) (creative midfield genius); Russell Brand (lanky, fast, sexy)

Forwards: Sooty (quiet destroyer); Sweep (translates Sooty's moves); Pete Doherty (knows how to score)

Subs: Amy Winehouse (wild card); Brucie (good game ... good game).

We can't lose.

Barry Tighe, Ilford, Essex

The Cornish group Fisherman's Friends recorded a song for the English World Cup team but most Cornish people were perplexed by this as Cornwall isn't truly English. The Cornish were more likely to support Mexico, Australia or South Africa. Johannesburg was once a largely Cornish city.

England? I don't think so. We didn't even have Nigel Martyn to claim – but I'm told Wayne Rooney is of Cornish descent so perhaps we can remain Fishermen's Friends after all.

Tim James, Penzance, Kernow

The England football team suffers from over-analysis paralysis, a problem well known to golfers who listen to far too much advice.

Paul Rose, Camberley, Surrey

Harry Redknapp the next England manager? Another one who'll have to learn the language!

Donald Coleman, Eynsham, Oxfordshire

After all his killing, corruption, land confiscation and oppression, Robert Mugabe finally committed a cardinal sin. He banned certain members of the press from entering his country – and thereby breeched an international cricket rule.

As a consequence of this dreadful crime, our cricketers decided to support democracy by saying that they would prefer not to play in Zimbabwe.

Our government set an excellent example of efficient decision-making in this matter – it's rumoured that the Sports Minister is still picking out the splinters from sitting on the fence.

Ron Daly, Nottingham

Giggs and Charlton have each played 606 league games now for Manchester United but how many minutes has each actually played? Substitutes weren't used in Charlton's career.

David Smith, Welton, Hull

Carlo Ancelotti says of Fernando Torres: 'He played well; he used his ability to move.' Translation: he managed to get onto the field unaided, remain upright for seventy-one minutes and got off again unaided.

Ronald Ball, Farnborough, Hampshire

Can you remember where you were when you heard about Wayne Rooney's ankle injury?

Mike Kirkup, Whitley Bay, Tyne & Wear

Could everyone please stop referring to Wayne Rooney's 'private life'. Nothing whatsoever about Wayne Rooney is private.

Godfrey H. Holmes, Chesterfield, Derbyshire

I have no sympathy whatsoever with our overpaid and overrated footballers. As a fairly senior member of staff in a secondary school officially classified by Ofsted as 'outstanding', I am yet to earn as much as Mr Rooney manages in his eight-week, football-free summer holiday – and I've been in my career for twenty-six years. His annual salary is more than the entire budget of my school, with well over 100 staff and 1,500 students.

When he retires from playing at the age of about thirty-five, a conservative estimate of his income would be £100 million, with about forty-five years to enjoy it. If I'm allowed to retire at sixty-five, I may be able to clear my mortgage by selling my modest house, buying a smaller one and using any pension lump sum to pay the balance. Government statistics suggest I will have fourteen months to enjoy it.

Mr Rooney could clear my mortgage in about nine days.

Chris Spark, Paignton, Devon

Why is it that whenever a football team has a bad run, the manager gets fired? It might not be his fault.

What about the striker who can't find the net with a sat nav? Or the defence with more holes than a golf course? Or even the keeper who always seems to be in the wrong place at the wrong time?

Shouldn't the whole picture be examined instead of automatically blaming the manager?

Wilbur Carpenter, Higham Ferrers, Northamptonshire

Football managers seem to be in the only professional body where the more you fail and the more often you're sacked, the more other teams want you – a sort of musical chairs for failures.

Brian Christley, Abergele, Conwy

If 'Butch' Wilkins were a stick of rock, he would have 'Chelsea' written all through him.

George Valentine, Rotherham, South Yorkshire

We have recently had several fairly major jobs carried out on our house and grounds. We had our old drive taken up and re-laid, some new windows fitted, a patio laid and a pergola over it as well as a leaking flat roof repaired.

Why can't British workmen take a leaf out of the customs and habits of footballers? When the jobs were finished, all the men did was take their money, thank me politely, clear the area thoroughly – and leave.

Where were the punches in the air? Where was the exchange of kisses on completion of the job they were paid to do? Where were the extravagant celebratory dances, the demonstrations and exaggerated gestures to our neighbours?

Have I been watching too much sport on television?

Peter Marriott, Nether Stowey, Somerset

I really feel sorry for soccer referee Howard Webb after his two hours of hell. Look at what he has to go through, running up and down, blowing a whistle and giving out yellow and red cards, while being verbally abused by the players. He must sometimes have wished he were dead.

A few months ago, I met a Chinese woman who had been trapped in earthquake rubble for twenty-eight hours. I'm sure she feels sorry for Howard Webb too.

Football these days is full of little boys wallowing in self-pity. Where have all the men gone? They fall down clutching their shins when they haven't been touched, hoping for a free kick. What sort of game is that, using lies to win?

Erle Montaigue, Cardiff

Beyond football

As a sixty-eight-year-old with a sixteen handicap you may say I don't know much about golf but if the powers that be want to encourage folk to take up the game, I think a couple of changes should be made.

As the wife and I sat down to watch the Ryder Cup, she asked why the players were taking so long to hit the ball. I tried to explain but to her the delay was just too long.

So I suggest we speed up this great game by making a rule that neither the player nor his caddie may go beyond his ball anywhere on the course and that a player has thirty seconds to play his or her shot providing it's safe to do so. This would make it a better spectator sport and encourage more viewers.

D. Capon, Dover, Kent

Let's bring back wrestling as a top sport. With all the energy and power our young boys and men seem to have, and no major war on which to vent their aggression, wrestling and boxing would be a legal way to rid themselves of all the testosterone channelled into troublemaking these days.

And perhaps taking part in a few wrestling bouts would calm down a few young women too.

Ann Allan, Seaford, Sussex

With the advent of Smell-o-Vision, when watching table tennis we'll be able to hear the ping and smell the pong.

David Manley, Las Palmas, Gran Canaria

Two years ago I was at the Wimbledon Men's Final, sitting a few rows behind the Royal Box, patiently awaiting the arrival of Nadal and Federer to come on court, when I heard 'rumblings' in the crowd. Boris Johnson had arrived! There was screaming, whooping and general merriment on seeing him take his seat.

He was smiling and shaking hands with other dignitaries in the Royal Box, totally unlike anything I've ever seen before, and when he turned around to wave at us all, the whole place just erupted. Every now and then, throughout the whole of the match, fans kept calling out his name in a friendly fashion, and sometimes Boris would respond with a turn or a wave. What a guy.

Oh, I say! What would Dan Maskell have made of that?

Mrs Sandra Wray, Collingham, West Yorkshire

A week ago, I visited my nearest DIY store and bought a children's DVD, a small hammer, six GU10 light bulbs and ten recordable CDs (with cases), all for £13. Last weekend, 700,000 people paid £14.95 to watch a one-sided boxing match that lasted three rounds.

Who got the better deal?

Chris Mawson, Denham, Suffolk

Ron Goodwin says he was told 10.10.10 was a lucky day so, at 10.10 a.m., placed ten pence each on four horses numbered 10 in an accumulator but none made the first three places.

He should have checked on how many of them came in tenth. He could have bet on that.

Dave Hough, Liverpool

On Easter Saturday there was a horse called Big Knickers in the 2 o'clock at Newton Abbot. I hope it wasn't put off by the shout of 'They're off!' at the start of the race.

Geoff Bonner, Newport Pagnell

It's amazing how athletics champions cease to win races after they come under suspicion for drug taking – no doubt due to the mental anguish they experience . . .

D. King, Bruton, Somerset

Why do the leaders in the London Marathon have to be hemmed in so tightly by motorcycles and that golf-cart thing? I can understand the need for cameramen but two bikes had only pillion passengers. It can't be much fun running twenty-six miles with lungs full of exhaust fumes.

A. Bailey, Shepherdswell, Kent

Reading about black-market tickets for international rugby matches, I'm left wondering who forces individuals to pay £100 for £35 tickets and who forces companies to part with £3,600 for six hospitality tickets?

The answer, of course, is that nobody does: it's their own free choice. It's the age-old law of supply and demand. If you value an event highly enough to pay over the odds for a ticket (as I have done numerous times in the past), you should be legally allowed to do so. I have no time for people who choose to pay out and then bleat about it afterwards.

S. C. H. Wing, Guildford, Surrey

The twisted tower

The Olympic Tower is aptly described as 'nineteen metres of twisted metal'. Whatever it is called, that is what it is and that is what it will always look like. This twisted, broken structure illustrates, for me, everything that is currently unsettling about the country's unstable situation.

Where is Prince Charles when you need him? This is one occasion when his intervention might be celebrated rather than criticised.

Sonia Stanford, Twickenham, Middlesex

After comparing it to France's Eiffel Tower, London Mayor Boris Johnson was unable to find words to describe our new Olympic monument. May I suggest the Awful Tower?

Gary Linley, Coleford, Gloucestershire

Under the hammer

Perhaps the greatest lesson the country could draw from the failed World Cup bid is to heed the observations of those abroad on the true state of Britain rather than continue to be in denial.

When the Russians commented on London's 'high crime rate' and 'high level of youth alcohol consumption' they made a fair observation. If as much effort were invested by politicians and state-funded quangos into dealing with these and other problems, so obvious to all who visit from abroad, as was put into a bid by the FA (staffed by a clearly dysfunctional leadership of ex-Labour apparatchiks), then in the mid-century when

England again bids for a global event, a more successful out-
come may result.

David von Ackerman, London SE16

In view of FIFA's now declared policy of taking the World Cup
to smaller, little known countries (like Qatar) would it not be
in the FA's interest to concentrate its efforts on making a joint
bid for 2026 in the name of Jersey and Guernsey? I'm sure it
would secure more than two votes.

Stephen Lockwood, Chichester, West Sussex

A matter of belief

On your knees

The suggestion by the C of E that churches should double up as shops or supermarkets is another bizarre, desperate gimmick by a Church that has totally lost its way.

Clearly, those who produce these ideas are totally uninfluenced by the Scriptures. Jesus drove the traders from the Temple saying, 'It is written, My house shall be called the house of prayer; but ye have made it a den of thieves.'

Is it too much to expect this Church to defend traditional teaching, particularly the Fourth Commandment which demands that Sunday should be kept holy as a day for the public and private worship of God and for the works of necessity and mercy?

Ronnie Crawford, Dromore, County Down

The fact that Pope John XXIII's body hasn't decomposed is seen as a sign of his sainthood. Lenin's body lay for years in Red Square without decomposition. Will the Roman Catholic Church soon be beatifying 'St Lenin'?

Keith Wiseman, Bury, Lancashire

I was astonished to hear how a junior FCO official had handled the Pope's visit and felt considerable sympathy for the Pope. But then the Vatican announced that Foreign Secretary David Miliband should have sacked the junior official rather than simply moving him to another parish . . .

Matthew Spencer, Bedford

No one should worry about having to go to confession: I have a long list of deaf priests to whom I direct my adult children. You can say what you like, they don't have a clue what you're saying but think it's lovely that you're there and will always absolve you. Should you see these deaf ones face to face, no need to worry, they usually have cataracts, too, so you're quite safe.

Once, one found what I said rather funny and the church building resounded loud and long with his laughter. I had been explaining the methods I used to steal my husband's beer, and describing its splendid qualities. I think he was even on the brink of asking me to get him some of this wonderful beer for him.

Mrs Catherine Venture, Erdington, Birmingham

I was baffled by the decision of Roman Catholic Church authorities in England and Wales to have a rap song as the 'Youth Anthem' during the papal visit to the UK.

Pope Benedict XVI has described pop music as 'the cult of the banal' and has stated that rock music 'is a form of worship . . . in opposition to Christian worship'.

Rap music has a beat with a downward deflection that is condescending by nature. It contains the essential rhythmic elements of bragging (*braggadocio*) and ritualized insult. Rap was largely influenced by rock 'n' roll (slang for sex) and has developed into trends of violence and gratuitous sex.

Putting Christian lyrics to such profane music doesn't make that music 'Christian'. This is inculturation gone haywire.

Paul Kokoski, Hamilton, Ontario

It has now been revealed that there is some secret hidden lettering in the eyes of the painting *Mona Lisa*. It's thought that two of the letters are a C and an E. It couldn't possibly be that the full lettering spells 'Made in China' could it?

Geoff Bonner, Newport Pagnell, Buckinghamshire

As for the burka . . .

Caroline Spelman would have us believe that it's 'empowering' for women who wear burkas 'to be able to chose each morning what they wear'. Would she care to comment on how many styles and colours of burkas are available for Muslim women to choose from?

Joseph Alexander, Sheffield

Caroline Spelman states that it is a woman's right to cover her face. If it's a person's right to cover, then it must be a person's right to uncover. I would like to be a nudist and walk the streets in the nude. I feel that I would be 'empowered' by doing this. Will Caroline Spelman support me in this right?

Harry King, Grimsby, Lincolnshire

I note that the Saudi princess who has a male model lover, and was allowing her flat to be used for a night of drink and drugs, arrived at court in a full face veil.

Clearly, her religious views are based on a 'selective' approach to Islamic law and teachings. Or was the burka being used as a disguise to avoid photographers? I doubt that we will hear that she is to face the wrath of the Islamic courts.

Carolo Guy, Chesterfield, Derbyshire

Present and past

Broken Britain?

We're told children's playgrounds are now 'too safe'. Now I know why one of our local kiddies' playgrounds was taken over by a huge group of teenagers during the summer holidays.

The foul-mouthed, obnoxious crowd wanted to be sure they were safe while they were on the swings and roundabout. All the mums kept the little ones away for fear of making it a 'no go' area for the teens. A building site would be a good option for them – they may all break their precious necks.

Rita Lampard, Leighton Buzzard, Bedfordshire

In my lunchbreak I went to the optician's to collect my new glasses. They were originally due last week but when I went to collect them I was told they were held up at the factory. I waited several minutes before an assistant approached me and, during the wait, listened to eighties' pop hits being piped around the shop. A man answered his mobile phone. He told the caller: 'I'm at the optician's.'

I ate lunch on a bench in Broadmead. Nearby, a man was shouting about the *Big Issue*, saying he had only one copy left. Young people were carrying clipboards and wearing tabards, trying to get passers-by to sign up for charity donations.

On my way back to the office, I tried to print a mini-statement from my bank's cashpoint but the screen said this was unavailable – the third day running that this had happened.

After work, I went home and picked up my post and checked my emails. I had received a letter from Plymouth, posted first class but which took three days to be delivered. My friend said his new neighbours had threatened to kill him because he'd painted his garden gate green. I received a monthly magazine by subscription, due five days ago.

After initial problems logging on to my email, I saw there was still neither a reply to my recent enquiry to a company, nor a response to my emails and letter to Crimestoppers enquiring about my bicycle, stolen in January.

I went to meet my father, who was stopping in Bristol for the evening, to break his train journey from London to Exeter. He had heard that if you travelled in the evening you could go all the way by train, rather than taking a coach part of the way because of track repairs.

He told me that one of his closest friends had died at the weekend. He had known her since they were at university in the 1950s. We went to a café where we chose vegetable soup from the menu but were told it wasn't available. The other customers were boisterous youths who occasionally swore.

As an experiment, we sent an email from one of Bristol's electronic information points. We thought this was a potentially amazing facility but found it fiddly and slow to use. While we were trying, a man came up and asked for twenty pence for a phone call.

We walked to Temple Meads station. In Queen Square, a

man with a blanket on his shoulders asked us to buy him a hot drink. The train was late. While we were waiting, a man asked us for money so he could pay to do voluntary work. We didn't understand his logic.

After my father had gone, I checked the bicycle racks on the platform, to see whether I could find my stolen bike. As I left the station, a youth asked me the way to McDonald's.

I walked back to College Green, where I had locked the bike that I had bought to replace my stolen one. Only the lock was left. I walked across to Bridewell Street police station to report this latest theft and on my way the man I'd met before asked me to buy him a hot drink.

I looked out for the bike, in case it was still in the area but the only cyclists were riding other bikes on the pavements, without lights.

The policewoman seemed sympathetic but said she couldn't cross-reference the theft with my previous theft, as it was being dealt with by another district. I had to give all my personal details again from scratch.

Another man in the police reception had been assaulted at the bus station. He was telling somebody about it on his mobile phone.

I walked home, looking out for either of my stolen bicycles on the way. As I crossed The Centre, the same man asked me yet again to buy him a hot drink.

By the Watershed, a man sitting under a blanket asked me to buy the *Big Issue*. When I got home, I sent an email to a magazine, to advertise the bike theft. There were problems sending the email but it went through on the third attempt.

I noticed that my flatmate had broken the light switch in the bathroom.

F. Harvis, Clifton, Bristol

Living in Hull, statistically one of the worst unemployment areas, I see many able-bodied men, particularly young ones, wandering around the streets doing nothing.

I'm sixty-five, recently retired, diabetic and have a serious heart condition. Needing some 'muscle' to help me clear an area and erect a new shed, I scanned the *Hull Daily Mail* small ads to get someone to give me a quote. Out of the fourteen I contacted:

- five didn't return phone messages to make appointments
- six made appointments but didn't turn up (two of them twice)
- one quoted £150 and said he would come back and confirm but never did
- one came and said that he couldn't put down the concrete slabs as he didn't know how so would send his mate, but no one else turned up
- one said he would consider it only if I sent him a photo of my garden.

So please don't let me hear too many stories of unemployment – there is work, and it may be closer than they think.

Carl Cassidy, Hull

We were promised a spectacular 'light show' resulting from the explosion of the giant star Betelgeuse. As this star was 640 light years from Earth, it must have exploded in 1371 and so no longer exists.

In 2651, inhabitants of a planet a similar distance away would see Earth as it is today and wonder if it contained intelligent life. Sorry folks.

John Haynes, Welford, Northamptonshire

The English are the most generous, hospitable people on earth – by law!

Michael Cooper, Shepperton, Middlesex

Let's face it

Sadly, Facebook has become a refuge for violent bullies, cowards and social outcasts. I finally decided to try to 'get down wiv da kids' and reluctantly joined the masses. However, after a couple of months of amusing myself by 'spying' on numerous friends and friends of friends I gave up.

Reading the crass remarks and inane comments of supposedly 'sensible' thirty-, forty- or even fifty-somethings was becoming more boring than watching the proverbial drying paint.

The internet is a potentially powerful force for good and is an inspiration to many but, alas, its darker side is as pernicious as the most potent drug.

Bridget Frew, Worthing, Sussex

Reading a disturbing account of a British soldier's 1995 tour of duty in Bosnia, I was nauseated by the horrific brutality inflicted on innocent people by their neighbours, by the very people they'd lived beside for generations and whom they believed they knew well.

But, even though I was disturbed by the harrowing idea that seemingly normal people could participate in such evil actions without remorse or compassion, I was smug in my belief that nothing like that could ever happen in the UK. The British people were just not like that.

Then I read the sinister comments on Facebook praising mad killer Raoul Moat – 35,000 of them!

And these were the tiny percentage with enough brainpower to switch on a computer and scratch a few incoherent words onto it.

Be afraid. Be very afraid . . .

Brendan O'Brien, Newport, South Wales

The youth today . . .

People have fifteen hours to make their vote. That should be sufficient and yet there's a proposal to extend it because some people are unable to plan their day in order to vote on time.

Many of those shown at closing time were teenagers with no responsibilities to take up their day. No doubt if there had been an incentive, such as a bar of chocolate or a lollipop, they would have got out of bed and been waiting for the polling station to open.

Peter A. Rushworth, Cullingworth, West Yorkshire

Things ain't wot they used to be

What a sad, frightening state of affairs exists on the Overslade estate in Rugby. What a contrast to the Overslade of the 1880s when the site was occupied by Overslade School. No trace remains of this preparatory establishment which once fed the great Rugby School itself.

I wrote about Overslade in a biographical essay on former schools inspector John Haslam. His uncle, John Monteith Furness was proprietor of Overslade School and Haslam was a pupil there. The school stood in eighteen acres, with a gymnasium and chapel, its fees were a whopping £85 a year (music and gymnastics extra).

This was, of course, a privileged world, where masters read Rider Haggard adventure stories to boys who would progress to public school and plum jobs in the machinery of the Empire. Who would wish a return to those days of inequality when poor children made do with the most rudimentary education before entering lives of hard work and low pay?

But with what horrors have we replaced it? Huge advances in post-war secondary education, years of social care, good housing and well-paid work haven't brought the quality of life or the security from crime or the hope for a better future. There are huge flaws in all these ideals and services and the feral youngsters of today's estate are the unfortunate result.

Idleness and poor examples of behaviour cause today's crimes. Money is no substitute for stable loving families, learning, employment and a cultivated sense of public duty and good behaviour. But money wisely spent is essential in solving the problems, particularly if we are to remove drugs and alcohol abuse from our communities, and end the easy choice of life on benefits without personal responsibility.

We take our true place in society only when we contribute to it through work and taxes and gain the self-esteem and respect of others that ought to be the mark of twenty-first century British society.

Graham Beard, Liverpool

A report about a rare Swedish Treskilling Yellow postage stamp reminded me of my stamp collecting as a twelve-year-old schoolboy. I was always searching for a stamp with a fault.

In 1941, during the reign of George VI, I discovered an orange 2d. stamp on which the letter o in the word 'postage' was filled in with white. In my young innocence, I excitedly wrote to Stanley Gibbons to find out if this stamp was worth more than its face value. Their reply stated that it depended on the interest of any philatelist.

I put the stamp away in my album and there is has remained for nearly sixty years. My stamp collecting days ended when I started an engineering apprenticeship with Sunbeam Talbot in 1944 but I still wonder if my faulty 2d. King George stamp would be of value to a collector.

R. A. E. Wood, Newark-on-Trent, Nottinghamshire

How sad that gentlemen who would like to offer a possibly pregnant lady a seat on public transport are now afraid to do so for fear of offending a possibly overweight lady who isn't pregnant at all.

When I worked in London in the early 1960s and travelled to work every day on the Underground, I was offered a seat by a distinguished-looking gentleman who insisted I take it. I was only twenty-one, very slim in those days, and only too pleased to smile thankfully and take the seat.

The distinguished-looking gentleman was Joe Grimond, leader of the Liberal Party. He made my day.

Jennifer Graeme, Shaldon, Devon

May I remind readers that 1 August is national White Glove Day, a day when we can remember by-gone eras and times when ladies were considered improperly dressed without their gloves.

Even in the summer, white cotton or lacy gloves were required to complete your outfits, and this applied to young girls too.

When I was a youngster, my mother wouldn't even take me shopping unless I was wearing my gloves. How times have changed.

Valerie Braithwaite, Harrow Weald, Middlesex

A Tarmac-ed path up Snowdon? What next, a stair lift on Everest?

Carol Owen, Chorley, Lancs.

Further to the inability of some people to hold a pen properly, I never cease to be appalled at the sight of poorly brought up people holding a knife as if they're holding a pen.

I can only assume that, as with crooking a little finger when drinking a cup of tea, they somehow imagine that it confers a degree of refinement. It most certainly does not and I urge anyone reading this who engages in either disgraceful practice to cease doing so immediately on pain of being marked down as an uneducated guttersnipe.

Roy Conolly, Haverfordwest, Pembrokeshire

I was sad to hear that, although the occasion was described officially as 'kissing hands', David Cameron on his appointment as prime minister broke with tradition and didn't actually kiss the Queen's hand, opting instead for a mere handshake.

A lovely, centuries-old gesture that expresses the

constitutional relationship beautifully was abandoned in the name, no doubt, of pointless and destructive 'modernisation'.

I remember a photo of a smiling Tony Blair kissing the Queen's hand graciously and on one knee. Why couldn't David Cameron have done the same?

Alan Kipps, Hadleigh, Essex

Anyone in doubt about the wording of the Magna Carta should visit Salisbury Cathedral, which has its own fine copy (plus a translation into English) – and you can even buy tea towels with it on in the cathedral shop.

Victoria Knollys, Salisbury, Wiltshire

I grew up in Lancing where rows of terraced houses have stood since the 1920s on land where market gardens had flourished in Victorian and Edwardian times. They grew grapes, peaches, lilies and other exotica for the London markets under glass in the summer sun.

When the carriage works arrived in the area, the market garden landowners sold out so housing could be built for the workers. Within a couple of decades, the works closed leaving Lancing with industrial-style streets. The wonderful fruit and flower gardens seem lost forever, limiting Lancing's potential as a holiday resort.

The promise of jobs often makes local councils sell out for a quick return, as they do to Tesco. But beauty and ambience can rarely be restored. Let's hope England can again be a paradise of fruit and flowers.

Rose 'Marg' Moloney, Lancing, Sussex

A pamphlet issued by the US War Department in 1942, entitled 'Instructions for American Servicemen in Britain 1942', includes the paragraph:

'The Briton is just as outspoken and independent as we are, but don't get him wrong. He is also the most law-abiding citizen in the world, because the British system of justice is just about the best there is. There are fewer murders, robberies and burglaries in the whole of Great Britain in a year, than in a single large American city.'

It's all changed in my lifetime. I'm seventy years old and look what has happened to our beautiful country; what have they done?

Robert Pierce, Glan Conwy, Colwyn Bay

In the Second World War, we had a slogan, 'Britain/London can take it'. It appears that it would be difficult to apply this to the present generation. The slightest upset in people's lives calls for counselling and/or compensation. I have a relative who was offered counselling because his car radio was stolen.

Policemen, firemen and soldiers see many unpleasant sights in the course of their duties but during the war many people, including children, saw appalling things that would make your hair curl. This was not only on the fighting fronts but also at home in the blitzed cities.

Were we tougher in the Forties or simply rougher and more ignorant? What do the psychologists think?

Mr M. F. Reid, St Albans, Hertfordshire

Don't decry the 'Blitz spirit'. I remember the bomb that fell in front of St Paul's Cathedral and the many bombs that fell on the city. My family and I had to sleep – or try to sleep – in a disused railway tunnel under Smithfield meat market. No bugs or lice were ever found there although we slept on the ground with other people all around. Later the Fox & Knox Mission helped to get bunk beds and a canteen going and formed a club down there. We even danced and did PE and made many new friends.

It wasn't all honey at that time but the 'Blitz spirit' really held us together and lasted for years to come. It's a great pity that the 'Blitz Spirit' doesn't exist today.

J. Fletcher, née Hambleton, Poplar, London E14

As a young lad in Skegness, Lincolnshire, from 1950 to 1952, I first 'worked' as a luggage barrow-boy, offering to barrow the luggage of holidaymakers arriving at Skegness Railway Station – the tips I received being far cheaper than taxi fares. This was a welcome boost to my pocket money and the enterprise continued on moving to Bridlington in 1952.

Then a pupil of Bridlington (Grammar) School for Boys, Saturday morning lessons were compulsory but as soon as school ended, I whizzed down to the nearby railway station, eager to start work. Needless to say, we weren't best friends with the taxi drivers.

One Saturday afternoon, while taking a family's bags to where they were staying, my form master rode by on his bicycle and recognised me. I thought nothing of it but the following Monday morning he asked to see me after class.

'Burrows,' he said, 'I saw you on Saturday afternoon barrowing luggage. I wouldn't have expected to see grammar school boys doing that kind of thing.' That was me ticked off for earning an honest crust. Sixty years on, it still makes me smile.

John Burrows, Humberstone, Leicestershire

Is it a sign of the times that, increasingly, mums waiting at primary school gates look more and more like the children's big sisters?

John Warren, Bexhill-on-Sea, East Sussex

Time please!

We live in beautiful Buckinghamshire with masses of 'country pubs' all around. But take away the chic eateries, the Balti horrors, the derelict closures, the plastic menus of brought-in, pre-packaged fare and the choice is minimal.

Time and again we struggle to find a traditional country pub, with real home-cooked food at sensible prices. The choice is very restricted.

Come on, landlords, let's get back to good old value for money and quality homemade food. Reverse the trend and you'll thrive again.

David M. Bernstein, High Wycombe, Buckinghamshire

Wouldn't we all like to find a comfortable, beamed country pub with reasonably priced food and drinks? Our local pub, a late-seventeeth-century masterpiece, has changed hands five times in the last thirteen years. The last tenant left when the brewery increased his rent to just less than £2,000 a week. Just imagine what his rates, his staff costs and other overheads are.

Food can be bought cheaply but the cost of preparation and waste must ultimately be reflected in the sale price. Drinks, if you're tied to a brewery, can't be bought cheaply.

Tony Dawson, Northill, Bedfordshire

Beyond the borders

Friend or foe

Our cleaner is from Poland and he's Magic. He asks people to call him Magic because that's how British people pronounce his name when they read it. But in another sense, he is magic – working seventy hours a week, Magic stacks shelves all night in Sainsbury's and in the early morning he cleans up after students in our halls of residence.

He's the friendliest man you could hope to meet first thing and perhaps the most British person I know. He adores our countryside (his favourite flower is the daffodil) and at Easter spent his wages travelling around Wales staying in B&Bs.

The majority of the immigration-sceptics aren't bigots, they just never get to see this side of immigration – that of a thoroughly decent man working in the dead of night doing jobs the natives wouldn't consider. More people in the country like him please.

Ashley Hall, Selwyn College, Cambridge

Forty years ago, I set out for India with three others – all of us recently trained journalists – in a specially adapted Land Rover. Our journey took us through Iran and Afghanistan.

Despite the grave misgivings of family and friends who viewed our trip as idiotic, we experienced nothing but friendship and kindness, especially in Afghanistan.

We towed a beaten up old VW beetle owned by a Kabul bank manager who was on a hunting expedition from just outside Dilaram to Kandahar, crossing the beautiful river Helmand, and then eventually on to his home in Kabul via Ghazni and Shaikhabad – a total distance of 450 miles.

For Afghanistan, this was one of the more peaceful periods in its history. There were no foreign forces in the country; tribal people lived in relative harmony and treated visitors with understanding and patience.

All that changed a few years later with the Russian invasion and now with Western troops across the country. Afghanistan should be allowed to make its own future. Do we never learn from history?

Robert Ian Brereton, Warminster

Centring on Europe

I have serious concerns about the sanity of MEPs following their decision to ban the sale of eggs by the dozen. Does the beleaguered taxpayer really have to fund such stupidity? Imagine trying to buy eggs using the new EU directive:

Shopkeeper: Good morning, madam. What can I get for you?

Shopper: I'd like some nice, fresh eggs please. My family is very fond of fresh boiled eggs.

Shopkeeper: Certainly madam. How many ... Oh! ... I mean how much would you like? ... In weight, that is.

Shopper: In weight? Well (pauses) enough for a family whose total body weight is about 465 kilograms.

Shopkeeper: Er . . .

At this point, any MEP with at least a modicum of common sense is invited to suggest what the shopkeeper says next.

Derek Hines, Crowborough, Sussex

A (retired) friend of mine has just returned from a holiday in Poland where his Polish wife was visiting her family. Their hotel claimed not to have received any reservation, despite copies of emails confirming the booking. While this was being sorted out, they went for a walk and found themselves outside the town hall.

Feeling mischievous, my friend told staff there that he had just arrived in Poland (true), was unemployed (technically true), had nowhere to stay (true) and under EU regulations he was entitled to accommodation and benefits. Apparently, the reply, issued forcefully, translated roughly as 'Depart!'

David Powell, Frimley, Surrey

European Central Bank chief Jean-Claude Trichet says, 'Pessimism over the eurozone is overblown'. In the immortal words of Mandy Rice-Davies, 'Well, he would say that, wouldn't he?'

Les Arnott, Sheffield

Looking across the pond

Should former President George W. Bush be considered 'illiperate'?

L. S. Filley, Dudley, West Midlands

I agree with those who recoil with horror at the thought of a UK presidency. To follow the likely catastrophe through to its worst possible conclusions, picture these possible scenarios:

Following the unexpected death of Harold Wilson, President Brown, after being sworn in, said: 'I am intoshicated at the idea of the fair and jusht shoshiety that we will build.'

After the richly deserved assassination of President Blair, President Prescott is photographed at a charming private inaugural party in the grounds of Buckingham Palace drinking tea from a Dresden saucer.

Finally, following a (God forbid) Labour landslide, President Kinnock, in his six-hour acceptance speech, made many startling new proposals, including the formation of a new Ministry of Feminine Affairs to be headed by his wife Glenys, at a modest salary of £5,000,000 per annum.

There's no need for change. Wise people know when they're well off.

John Creais, Sidcup, Kent

It was interesting to read the views of that prominent academic Charlotte Church in her condemnation of George Bush for his supposed lack of geographical knowledge.

I feel compelled to point out that if there is any ignorance in this matter, it lies with her, not him. Had she known as much about American geography as she should have known before condemnation of one of its citizens, Charlotte would have known that there are many small townships in America named Wales – in fact there's one not too far from the Bush holiday home in Massachusetts.

Celebrities should get their brains in gear before belittling others.

Sheila Essery, Caversham, Berkshire

First or second degree murder? Surely murder is murder. Just as with pregnancy and integrity: one can't be a bit pregnant or have some integrity; either one is pregnant or one is not, either one has integrity or one does not.

Do we really want to follow America on this?

Garry Howes, Wokingham

Comparing 'moral Americans' with 'English yobs' is like comparing apples and oranges. There are many moral, decent, well-behaved English people, just as in America there are drunken yobbish 'trailer trash' types.

More to the point, while English football hooligans might be feared overseas, most countries gladly welcome British troops. The same cannot be said of the American army which behaves like a bunch of undisciplined yahoos, is totally unaware of who their enemy is and even seems incapable of aiming at the correct target.

Unfortunately, the 'moral majority' of America seems unable to influence its military.

D. J. Tyrer, Southend-on-Sea, Essex

I can vouch for those who say attending an American baseball game is paradise compared with an English football match.

When we stayed with friends in Denver, they treated us to a visit to watch the Denver Broncos at the Mile High Stadium in the city, a really thrilling experience with a great atmosphere and a capacity crowd filling the stadium. We saw people going to the various bars and bringing glasses of beer back to their seats but there was not one instance of drunkenness.

I hate to think what it would have been like if it had been here. After the game, everyone left in an orderly manner with no pushing or shoving and no foul language was heard throughout the whole day. So, better stupid Americans than British lager louts.

Mr J. N. Bennett, Folkestone, Kent

There certainly are different attitudes towards drinking between here and across the pond. After three days in Chicago, having done a lot of sightseeing, my wife and I asked our tour guide directions to a few bars where we might catch the odd blues combo and have a beer or two.

She replied, rather curtly: 'Well, sir, as I'm only nineteen and too young to drink I wouldn't know that, would I?'

Mark O'Keefe, Stockport

Mindful that, in America, more people get on a bus crash than get off it (suffering from whiplash), President Obama's rhetorics about BP and the oil spill will produce open season for many fishermen who in truth weren't doing very well.

Philip Pearce-Smith, Holbury, Hampshire

Geographically speaking

As a Middlesex man, born and bred, I'm still smarting from the abolition of the county in 1967. To see Staines described as a 'Surrey town' really rankles – Surrey is south of the Thames; Staines is north of it – and a fine town it is. It doesn't need a name change.

Some years ago, astrologer Russell Grant began a campaign to reinstate Middlesex as a county. It worked with Rutland, why not with Middlesex?

John Adams, Shaftesbury, Dorset

I can't be alone in being increasingly irritated by the incorrect use of the term 'the UK'. The UK is a political representation of our four countries – England, Wales, Scotland and Northern Ireland – it has no geographical meaning. It entails these representative countries at, for instance, the United Nations when the British people's views are expressed as one. We are British, not UK-ish.

These days, it's 'the UK this', 'the UK that' – which is incorrect. Use of the term is particularly vexing in connection with weather forecasts. When rain is given for the 'south' of the UK, does this mean England, Wales, Scotland or Northern Ireland? People return to the UK from abroad. Why don't we say 'England', for example, – or are we frightened we may somehow offend?

Mr W. G. Humphreys, Cowes, Isle of Wight

Learning stuff

School reports

I took my six-year-old granddaughter, Lucy, to school when her mother was ill and was amazed at how disorganised her school is. She's already lost an expensive jacket, despite it having a name-tape inside and I went into her classroom before school started and found the children watching television, instead of playing outside.

The next day, Lucy came out without yet another jacket, so I insisted on going into her cloakroom to find it. I discovered that she'd been excluded from her PE lesson and had to sit on her own in the corner because she couldn't find her PE kit. Surely, a six-year-old shouldn't be embarrassed and excluded because the school doesn't have a proper system?

Lucy explained that there were too many children in her class for the number of coat-hooks, each hook had four coats on it, so it was difficult to find her coat at home-time and that she couldn't keep track of her PE kit.

When I was a schoolgirl (many years ago, I admit), we each had our own coat-hook for our coat and PE kit.

I don't have a great deal of money but I think I need to spend what I do have on Lucy's education; she's a bright child who tells me school is 'boring'. For a six-year-old to say that, says it all.

Sandra Thurgood, Laugharne, Carmarthenshire

Mention of three flying ducks on the wall of every working class home took me back to my school days at St Bartholomew's Grammar School in Newbury in the 1960s.

Even to this day I very rarely win anything in a raffle but at this particular speech day and prize-giving ceremony, after many other winning tickets, one of my numbers came up. Having seen other boys win good-looking prizes, I went forward full of expectation.

The teacher in charge picked up from a now rather sparse table of prizes a set of three flying ducks attached to a piece of card. With some dexterity he used a pair of scissors to cut one away and present it to me.

Strangely, he didn't comment on my look of disappointment as my not-yet-fully-stiff upper lip quivered.

Bill Martin, Cowes, Isle of Wight

I've known for some time that school bags make you lopsided.

Dennis Tilt, Bookham, Surrey

It would appear that our schools are simply not teaching our children to read. My 'slightly dyslexic' (whatever that means – it's the primary school's label, not mine) son was eventually taught to read properly by the use of phonics at the age of eleven, following his 'inability to catch on' while surrounded by colourful books in the classroom.

His private tutor, a retired head teacher, informed us that our son had never been taught to read, something he rectified within six months. At considerable cost, we then took him out of the state secondary school system to enable him to sit his A-levels at grammar school.

Our son went on to gain a BSc in electrical engineering before attending college in America to qualify as a computer animator. He attended primary school back in the late 1980s – and it seems nothing has changed.

Rosina Brown, Westgate, Kent

Max Hastings tells us that 'the Common Entrance exam, which every public school applicant must sit at thirteen, really counts. Eton, Radley, Winchester, St Paul's, simply will not admit stupid pupils, even if they're dukes' sons'.

Well, perhaps not 'a duke's (stupid) son' – but one of these acclaimed schools did admit the 'stupid' son of a prince, though to my astonishment, few seemed to notice at the time the sneaky way in which this was done.

When Prince Harry, known to be academically challenged, was due to leave Ludgrove prep school and move on to secondary education, he was clearly never going to be able to pass the Common Entrance exam to join his brother at Eton and an announcement was made that Harry would remain at Ludgrove for an extra year. By amazing coincidence, that same year, Eton decided that in future it would also admit pupils on the basis of their sporting prowess, rather than academic skills.

The following year, Harry – an excellent sportsman – was able to join William at Eton after all, a decision which actually did the boy no favours as he always trailed miserably behind everyone else in the classroom and ultimately left Eton with poor A-level results.

Does Eton still admit sporty, non-academic pupils, I wonder?

Donna Kellie, Wolverhampton, West Midlands

I suspect Stella McCartney said what she did about private schooling because she's afraid of the opinions of her champagne-drinking New Labour friends.

As a mother, she wants to give her children the best possible start in life, hence the expensive private schools. Accompanying this with the suggestion that she'll send them to state schools if they start talking in posh accents is supposed to placate (often rich) people, who hate private schools and any notion of being posh.

I'd have more respect for her if she simply told her friends she was doing the best for her children and that if they have a problem with that then they are clearly no friends of hers.

Also, if her children develop posh accents and she sends them to a state school, won't they just get beaten up?

Adeyemi Banjo, London SE15

I worked hard at my GCSEs and achieved eleven A* grades. I pushed myself even harder for A-levels, choosing to take five, and was rewarded with A* in English, Religious Studies and Theatre Studies and As in History and Classics.

Last year, before my final results came through, I applied to take English at five universities but received not one conditional offer. This year, I applied again to five universities to study

English, believing perhaps they were wary of offering me a place last year because of concerns about my performing arts interests clashing with my studies. I've just received my fifth rejection.

I wonder now why I bothered to work so hard to achieve the grades I did. All the effort and distress seems pointless. I read in the press yet again that all the university places are going to private school pupils. I attended a private school until my GCSE year but it doesn't seem to have helped me.

I guess I'll just have to be a stripper.

Lucy Ogilvie, address supplied

Woodwork, Latin, lace . . .

As a craft teacher who came from industry with qualifications to train and obtain a teaching certificate in the sixties, it soon became clear that craft teachers were deemed to be 'second-class citizens' in the teaching world.

The world of craft involved woodwork, metalwork, needle-work, domestic science, technical drawing and art, and offered real, hands-on practical skills. My academic colleagues couldn't understand the importance of practical subjects, although crafts support and re-enforce in real terms the academic subjects such as Mathematics, Science and English. Yes, we held tests and examinations but still without gaining my academic colleagues' acceptance (in fact some found it highly amusing to declare that they couldn't wire an electric plug or put up a shelf).

At that time, all pupils of all abilities left school with good practical knowledge and skills.

I believe that academic pressure has promoted what I call a 'practical-illiterate group of citizens'. In this day and age, when mechanical and hand tools can easily be purchased and used, the teaching of safe practical skills is of vital importance. Real hands-on teaching is costly but in the long term it will benefit our future citizens.

Arthur Goddard, Newark, Nottinghamshire

Education Secretary Mr Gove wants Latin to be taught in our schools. Who will teach it? How are we going to train these teachers? How will we train the inspectors who will have to judge the lessons. Is the man *stultus*?

Mr M. H. Day, Hucknall, Nottinghamshire

Schools could play more of a part in exposing children to classical music. When I was at primary school in the late sixties/early seventies, a teacher, Mrs Crudgington, would play classical music on the piano as we came into assembly. The name of the piece and the composer would be written on a board beside the piano.

I remember particularly liking *The Entrance of the Queen of Sheba* by Handel and requested this to be played when I got married in the nineties.

Sarah Barron, Wimbledon

The paradox of the '3Rs' is that the earlier you stuff them down the throat, the less likely is their digestion. Einstein didn't read until after his eighth birthday.

Finland, Germany and other countries now more advanced than ours, don't even begin to teach reading before seven. They know, as all teachers used to know, that nature requires foundations to be built before the cognitive window opens at around age seven.

Many children do develop faster but the rule used to be that the longer you leave the mind to do its own thing, the richer will be the result – as with Einstein.

The disadvantaged child needs stories, games and social interaction in a language-rich environment, not the brutal assault of synthetic phonics.

Grethe Hooper Hansen, Bath

I'm very sorry to hear that the City & Guilds Certificate in Lacemaking is being withdrawn. This is a catastrophe for lacemaking in Britain. Where will we turn to in future for standards of good practice in this craft?

Lacemaking lessons are already being withdrawn in further education, due to the withdrawal of government concessions and the fact that the lessons are at the wrong times: 10 to 12 p.m. or 2 to 4 p.m. when most people are at work.

On the continent you can go to university for five years to study lacemaking. In France, from eight years of age you can go to your local lace school, at no cost, to start learning about lace and lacemaking. In England we have nothing of this kind.

In the age of the 'throwaway society', maintaining the skills of all old crafts is very important, cost effective and part of our history. Lacemaking in this country has been a tradition for many, many years but the tradition will die if there is no one to teach it. It may seem a small thing but it will be an important loss to our children's children.

Elizabeth Turnbull Welch, Littlebourne, Kent

The story of Richard Rudd who indicated to his family by blinking his eyes that he wanted to live, struck a chord with me because I've often thought that if I was in the same situation, I would be able to hold a conversation with anyone who could read Morse.

There must still be hundreds of radio amateurs like me who could do the same. What a shame that the Morse code is no longer seen as a valuable means of communication.

Harry Kennard, Peasmarsh, Rye

A GCSE in brushing your teeth? Presumably you'll have to pass the oral.

Mr P. J. Taylor, Sutton in Craven, West Yorkshire

It's not just what you say . . .

You what?

Andrew Hamer and Fritz Spiegl think the cleaner air now enjoyed by Liverpudlians has reduced the Scouse accent. As a speech therapist with thirty-five years of experience in treating thousands of Liverpool children with speech and language disorders, I query their findings. If a polluted atmosphere causes adenoidal speech, why is it that people living in Sheffield, Birmingham and Manchester (which had much more heavy industry than Liverpool) show few signs of adenoidal speech?

The cause of adenoidal tones (apart from adenoids and colds) is unclear, though some experts say tension in the pharynx can induce a lack of nasality. Messrs Hamer and Spiegl's views are largely subjective. I'm not aware of any established test to determine the amount of adenoidal tones used by an individual.

No accent is governed by tone alone but by misuse in pronouncing consonants, vowels, diphthongs and triphthongs. Cilla Black's 'a lorra lorra laughs' is a good example. Many Scousers will take off 'thur fur gloves to pay thur fur on the bus'.

Social mobility, the popularity of television soaps and the influence of newsreaders affect many accents and all speech patterns change with time. Dialects (the use of certain words exclusive to an area) are dying out in many parts of the country but I doubt if Scouse will go the same way.

William Good, Liverpool

What better example for the argument against regional accents on national TV than Quincy Jones trying to understand Jason Manford and Alex Jones on *The One Show*? A bit embarrassing.

Terry Isted, Portsmouth

Have a nice day

Having lived in the USA, I find their 'Have a nice day' genuine, and they usually substitute 'afternoon' or 'evening' for the 'day', when relevant.

Why would anyone call it insincere drivel and assume everyone loathes it? It's absurd for anyone to get a bee in their bonnet about this in a country where people frequently squawk 'See yer la'er'.

John Smith, Kings Lynn, Norfolk

Having watched a few talent show episodes on television, I'm curious to know why all of the participants sing with phoney American accents, while the vast majority speak Estuary English, with the accompanying glottal stop. Does anyone know the reason for this strange practice?

Ivor Kowalczyk, Berwick Hill, Northumberland

Gosh, I'm glad I'm not an American, what with all that 'hunkering down' and other such Neanderthal expressions . . .

Joe Gibson Dawson, Chorley, Lancashire

The admirable Quentin Letts has developed a bee in his bonnet regarding use of words like the American 'airplane' instead of 'aeroplane'. Quite right too. But he may be too late.

It's now just about impossible to scan newspaper City pages without reading about rates being 'hiked' – although rates do not go for long walks in this country, they are raised.

On the sports pages, footballers are said to have been 'hooked'. I could nominate several of their number who should be subjected to this painful indignity but when I consulted a ten-year-old American of my acquaintance I learnt that it meant substituted.

I realize that a language must evolve or it stagnates but it doesn't seem necessary to adopt a new one almost overnight. If we have to go down that road, can we at least have French? So much more elegant than American.

Martin Lewis, London N7

I'm sick of the greeting 'Hi there'. I refuse to be greeted in this manner and tell shop assistants and any others who may address me so.

No, I don't do 'Hi', not being an American, I do 'Hello' or 'Good morning', 'Good afternoon' or 'Good evening'. We have a wonderful English language and don't need such imports.

Nor do I respond to 'Regular coffee'. I have large, medium or small. And the latest stupid and meaningless comment is

'Enjoy'. What, in heaven's name, does that mean? Let's preserve our language.

Mrs F. Read, Bristol

For the love of words

Quote of the week, by Education Secretary Michael Gove, while being interviewed about the student demos by an excitable female presenter who appeared to support the violence and was being uppity: Mr Gove, with a laugh '. . . I think you may have taken too many Paxman pills . . .' What a put-down!

Jack Roberts, High Wycombe

Luddite delight: Apple and BlackBerry crumble.

Paul Key, Arnold, Nottinghamshire

What logic is there in going all the way to Mars to bring back a sample of earth . . . ?

Joseph G. Dawson, Withnell, Chorley, Lancashire

Why all the talk about 'cuts to the defence budget'? We don't have a defence budget – for the last few years all we've had is an attack budget.

Mr P. R. North, Brigg, Lincolnshire

Jobsworths: one of these pointless people recently told our market egg-seller that his 'jumbo eggs' description was illegal as the eggs had no relation to elephants. Honestly. Has he told Boeing?

How do we get rid of these people?

Pat Noujaim, Aylesbury

What does 'means testing' mean? It means those who pay nothing get everything and those who pay everything get nothing. How fair is that?

Andrew Hinton, Swansea

Further to the fate of the village sign at Shitterton, we have friends who are retiring to France. They will be moving to Condom. I wonder how often that sign has been removed by English visitors.

Richard Strother, Southampton

Before returning home after spending a holiday with us, a German student asked: 'Why do the English speak English so badly?' A carn imagine wha' 'e meant by tha' like, or where 'e go' tha' idea from, yer know wharra mean.

Jim Reed, Hartlepool

If a monarch is dethroned and a bishop is defrocked, how might people in other trades and professions be similarly dispatched?

Might an exorcist be demented? Or an examiner detested? Perhaps a disc jockey would be defunked, a sailor desalinated and a nursery nurse decried. Would a train driver be derailed or a chef deserted?

At least, in writing this, I cannot be considered unlettered.

George North, Lechlade, Gloucestershire

Wee reed a dissterbing reeport that Heinz R 2 spend millions rebranding their 'beans' as 'beanz.' They've now lost at leest won cusstomer as eye reefuze to eet anything that iz incorreckt-ly spellt.

Graham Shakeshaft, South Brent, Devon

In a simulated terror attack staged at the NEC, the emergency services took two hours to respond. Isn't this taking realism a bit too far?

Mr S. Eaton, Solihull

Oxymoron collection

Surely the most relevant oxymoron for these times is 'help desk'.

Margaret White, Bourne End, Buckinghamshire

How about 'amicable divorce'?

Sandy Pratt, Lingfield, Surrey

I saw a classic oxymoron when I was out recently – white lilac!

Joy Webb, Gillingham, Kent

The ultimate oxymoron must be 'Tony Blair, peace envoy'.

Richard Claxton, Fritton, Norfolk

Surely a 'secret to tell on Twitter' must be the ultimate oxymoron.

Audrey Long, Barnstaple, Devon

One of the best oxymorons is 'affordable housing'.

David Stuckey, Stevenage, Herts.

The ultimate oxymoron has got to be 'traveller community'.

David Brent, Ashford, Kent

The ultimate oxymoron is 'lovable rogue' of which my home town has more than its fair share.

Ray Williams, Anfield, Liverpool

The most glaring oxymoron these days is 'low-cost airline'.

Val Fish, Werrington, Cambridgeshire

Oxymoron? How about 'high-class prostitute'?

Raymond Briars, Poole, Dorset

Now that we have so many politicians and trade union leaders who purport to be economics experts even though they didn't see the crash coming, 'left wing intellectual' is my favourite oxymoron.

Ray Robinson, London SE9

My favourite oxymoron is 'public servant'. It always makes me laugh when I hear that one.

Rod Crisp, Hunstanton, Norfolk

An oxymoron heard by everyone in the city is the 'loud murmur' of rush-hour traffic.

Ron Watson, Hexham, Northumberland

If cattle were found to be very intelligent, would the ultimate oxymoron then be a 'moron ox'?

Bob Bailey, Bristol

Oxymorons? Enough already.

J. A. Scurfield, Durham